Helene Lange, Louis Richard Klemm

Higher Education of Women in Europe

Helene Lange, Louis Richard Klemm

Higher Education of Women in Europe

ISBN/EAN: 9783744776370

Printed in Europe, USA, Canada, Australia, Japan

Cover: Foto ©Suzi / pixelio.de

More available books at **www.hansebooks.com**

HIGHER EDUCATION OF WOMEN
IN EUROPE

BY

HELENE LANGE
BERLIN

TRANSLATED AND ACCOMPANIED BY COMPARATIVE STATISTICS
BY L. R. KLEMM, Ph. D.

NEW YORK
D. APPLETON AND COMPANY
1890

International Education Series

EDITED BY
WILLIAM T. HARRIS, A. M., LL. D.

VOLUME XVI.

INTERNATIONAL EDUCATION SERIES.

Edited by W. T. Harris.

It is proposed to publish, under the above title, a library for teachers and school managers, and text-books for normal classes. The aim will be to provide works of a useful practical character in the broadest sense. The following conspectus will show the ground to be covered by the series:

I.—History of Education. (A.) Original systems as expounded by their founders. (B.) Critical histories which set forth the customs of the past and point out their advantages and defects, explaining the grounds of their adoption, and also of their final disuse.

II.—Educational Criticism. (A.) The noteworthy arraignments which educational reformers have put forth against existing systems: these compose the classics of pedagogy. (B.) The critical histories above mentioned.

III.—Systematic Treatises on the Theory of Education. (A.) Works written from the historical standpoint; these, for the most part, show a tendency to justify the traditional course of study and to defend the prevailing methods of instruction. (B.) Works written from critical standpoints, and to a greater or less degree revolutionary in their tendency.

IV.—The Art of Education. (A.) Works on instruction and discipline, and the practical details of the school-room. (B.) Works on the organization and supervision of schools.

Practical insight into the educational methods in vogue can not be attained without a knowledge of the process by which they have come to be established. For this reason it is proposed to give special prominence to the history of the systems that have prevailed.

Again, since history is incompetent to furnish the ideal of the future, it is necessary to devote large space to works of educational criticism. Criticism is the purifying process by which ideals are rendered clear and potent, so that progress becomes possible.

History and criticism combined make possible a theory of the whole. For, with an ideal toward which the entire movement tends, and an account of the phases that have appeared in time, the connected development of the whole can be shown, and all united into one system.

Lastly, after the science, comes the practice. The art of education is treated in special works devoted to the devices and technical details useful in the school-room.

It is believed that the teacher does not need authority so much as insight in matters of education. When he understands the theory of education and the history of its growth, and has matured his own point of view by careful study of the critical literature of education, then he is competent to select or invent such practical devices as are best adapted to his own wants.

The series will contain works from European as well as American authors, and will be under the editorship of W. T. Harris, A. M., LL. D.

Vol. I. **The Philosophy of Education.** By JOHANN KARL FRIEDRICH ROSENKRANZ. $1.50.

Vol. II. **A History of Education.** By Professor F. V. N. PAINTER, of Roanoke, Virginia. $1.50.

Vol. III. **The Rise and Early Constitution of Universities.** With a Survey of Mediæval Education. By S. S. LAURIE, LL. D., Professor of the Institutes and History of Education in the University of Edinburgh. $1.50.

Vol. IV. **The Ventilation and Warming of School Buildings.** By GILBERT B. MORRISON, Teacher of Physics and Chemistry in Kansas City High School. 75 cents.

Vol. V. **The Education of Man.** By FRIEDRICH FROEBEL. Translated from the German and annotated by W. N. HAILMANN, Superintendent of Public Schools at La Porte, Indiana. $1.50.

Vol. VI. **Elementary Psychology and Education.** By JOSEPH BALDWIN, Principal of the Sam Houston State Normal School, Huntsville, Texas. $1.50.

Vol. VII. **The Senses and the Will.** Observations concerning the Mental Development of the Human Being in the First Years of Life. By W. PREYER, Professor of Physiology in Jena. Translated from the original German, by H. W. BROWN, Teacher in the State Normal School at Worcester, Mass. Part I of THE MIND OF THE CHILD. $1.50.

Vol. VIII. **Memory.** What it is and how to improve it. By DAVID KAY, F. R. G. S. $1.50.

Vol. IX. **The Development of the Intellect.** Observations concerning the Mental Development of the Human Being in the First Years of Life. By W. PREYER, Professor of Physiology in Jena. Translated from the original German, by H. W. BROWN, Teacher in the State Normal School at Worcester, Mass. Part II of THE MIND OF THE CHILD. $1.50.

Vol. X. **How to Study Geography.** By FRANCIS W. PARKER. Prepared for the Professional Training Class of the Cook County Normal School. $1.50.

Vol. XI. **Education in the United States.** Its History from the Earliest Settlements. By RICHARD G. BOONE, A. M., Professor of Pedagogy in Indiana University. $1.50.

Vol. XII. **European Schools.** Or what I saw in the Schools of Germany, France, Austria, and Switzerland. By L. R. KLEMM, Ph. D., Author of "Chips from a Teacher's Workshop," and numerous schoolbooks. $2.00.

Vol. XIII. **Practical Hints for the Teachers of Public Schools.** By GEORGE HOWLAND, Superintendent of the Chicago Schools. $1.00.

Vol. XIV. **Pestalozzi: His Life and Work.** By ROGER DE GUIMPS. Authorized translation from the second French edition, by J. RUSSELL, B. A., Assistant Master in University College School, London. With an Introduction by Rev. R. H. QUICK, M. A.

Vol. XV. **School Supervision.** By J. L. PICKARD, LL. D.

EDITOR'S PREFACE.

The battle for the higher education of women has been fought in this country, but we can not yet say that it has been fought out. Up to the generation of men now living the question had not been agitated. The few instances of institutions attempting collegiate instruction of women, and the still fewer experimenting with co-education in colleges, were not accepted as forerunners of a movement likely to become general. The majority of public high schools throughout the country thirty years ago and the normal schools were testing by co-education the relative ability of girls to pursue secondary studies in the same classes with boys. The result is well known. The girls proved their capability to perform the same intellectual tasks as boys. What they lacked at first in the qualities of originality and assimilative power they made up in memory and delicacy of appreciation. Many girls excelled the average boy even in originality. Alertness and versatility were manifested from the first—the well-known discriminations which were urged by Dr. Clarke many years ago against what he called "identical co-education." He described the female characteristics as versatility and periodicity, while the male sex possessed persistence and strength. It was thought that these distinctions rendered the education of the sexes together in the same classes undesirable and impracticable. Experience has not, however, confirmed the theory. The differences of mind, on the whole, when brought to bear on the subjects studied in the college or university, tend rather to help than to hinder the progress of both sexes. Each party gains something from the other one's views, and, although the profit of higher study is not precisely the same for women as for men, there is ample profit for each. Hence co-education in college work makes progress continually, and the higher education of women in one of the two modes —in separate institutions or in co-educating ones— is become quite a matter of course.

Whatever we are accustomed to seems to have the ground all to itself as against a newly proposed innovation. The unusual appears absurd. But a generation of people who have lived through more than one radical change of custom gets submissive to destiny and hears of new social schemes with composure. It does not dare to trust any longer its sense of the absurd, having learned that manners and customs strange to us always seem absurd, and that what we practice as the most natural and proper thing in the world would have seemed to our grandparents the height of the ridiculous.

Immediate likes and dislikes, based on taste or

habit, are therefore set aside instinctively by us, and we endeavor to judge impartially the new order proposed, and decide its claims on rational grounds.

What are the grounds for this change of opinion on the subject of the higher education of women? Has it always been a desideratum under all stages of civilization, or is it only a new thing incident to a new order of human development and just now become possible? Or is it perhaps an incident to some passing phase of historical growth, and destined to disappear as suddenly as it arose?

The question of education has reference to vocation and destiny, for it is a process of preparation for an end. The education of woman involves the theory of the life sphere of woman. Again, education must be of two kinds—general, fitting each individual for his common destiny with all, giving him participation with all mankind in the heritage of human experience and wisdom that has accumulated; special, as fitting each individual for the particular calling he shall occupy.

A study of social and national development will, I think, make clear the grounds for customs that have prevailed in female education, and prove conclusively that the new social conditions of the present and future demand higher education for woman.

In the first place, we must note the fact that the education of the people as people is itself quite a modern thing in history. The victory of productive industry over nature by the aid of machinery is itself both cause and effect of democracy. In the primitive conditions of society man is not able to provide for food, clothing, shelter, and culture except by the formation of rigid castes. When natural science has come and invention has secured the co-operation of the physical forces of nature so as to emancipate man from drudgery to some degree then begins the abolition of caste, not by the degradation of the higher classes, but by the elevation of the lower into higher castes.

It is this process which characterizes our present civilization. Education is its most important word, because in this is found the means of elevating the individual from a lower to a higher caste.

With the emancipation of the industrial classes, we have arrived at the new question of the emancipation of women so far as sex has produced caste limitations in the past. Let us examine these ideas more in detail.

There are three epochs of historic growth or social evolution which must be studied in order to understand the necessity for the higher education of women that has asserted itself in this age.

I. First, there, is the savage state of man, in which the two sexes fall into an antithesis whose extremes are drudge and warrior. The education of woman in this period consists in acquiring a knowledge of a few arts and dexterities, including the preparation of food, clothing, and shelter, and the care of the family. The man, on the other hand, gives his whole attention to the war and the chase. Hunting is, in fact, the only one of the civil occupations which is a training for war. The borderland of the savage tribe is so near the center of his territory, and his diplomacy is so insufficient to manage the interests of peace with surrounding tribes that he can not sleep in security a single night. He must be always on the alert, practicing the arts of war and ready by night and by day to repel attack. The savage man is defender and law-giver, the savage woman brings up the family and attends to the industries.

II. *The Division of Labor.*—The incorporation of tribes into nations brings about the second stage of society—that in which man is relieved from military duty to a great extent. His border-land is removed to a distant frontier, and soldiery becomes one of the special vocations which a few persons engage in. The great majority of men learn the arts of peace, and division of labor begins. Woman now leaves the sphere of the arts and trades wherein most division of labor exists, and retires within the family, working at the final processes of preparation for immediate consumption—such as cooking, sewing, mending, and the innumerable arts that go under the name of "housework" and the care of helpless children or helpless aged.

III. *The Age of Machinery.*—The era of productive industry has two distinct epochs. In the first there is such specialization of industry that each laborer tends to become a mere hand, performing a merely mechanical result requiring a minimum of directive intelligence in its performance. In the second epoch, labor-saving machinery takes the place of the human hand, and the individual laborer ascends to the higher vocation of director or manager of a machine. He uses intelligence, works with his brain, where before he worked with his muscles alone.

In the first epoch, that of the division of labor, there prevails a tendency toward infinite subdivision. Each special industry is divided and subdivided again until it seems as though purely mechanical labor, entirely devoid of mental effort, would finally be reached. With each step toward subdivision and specialization the simplicity of the labor increases, and it finally becomes easy to invent a machine propelled by the blind forces of nature to take the place of the human machine. The mechanical occupation of the man is now gone, and he has left for him the task of connecting and disconnecting the active power (steam, water, electricity, etc.) with the machine, and of directing its operation upon the material to be elaborated.

With the first invented machines, only the physical labor requiring the most brute strength or mechanical application is conquered, and transferred from the hand to the machine. A great deal of hand labor, however, still remains in the process of directing the application of the machine. The further progress of invention adds more machinery to still further emancipate the hand, in this direction and application of machinery to the material to be manufactured. There arises a constant emancipation of the individual from mere manual labor and a continual change of vocations from those requiring mechanical skill toward those requiring intellectual versatility. Not physical strength, nor manual skill developed through the long years of apprenticeship, is required in the epoch of labor-saving machinery. The time required for apprenticeship continually shortens, and the demand for ready-educated intelligence grows more imperative.

Even in our day and generation, early as it is in the era of development of productive industry by labor-saving machinery, we all recognize the advantage which the versatility of educated intelligence possesses over the skill of the mere hand laborer, acquired through a seven years' apprenticeship and a score of years of journeymanship. The mere hand laborer, skillful and industrious though he be, is continually thrown ashore on the strand of pauperism, because his occupation is gone. A newly invented machine now performs his labor at so small a cost to society that the human machine, in competition with the other, can not earn his food and clothing. What is left for the individual who has survived his vocation? He must enter a new one. After twenty or thirty years of apprenticeship and journeymanship all his muscles have become set in the direction of special manipulations required in his trade, and he can not acquire the new manipulations necessary to a new trade with the same facility of adaptation that belonged to him in early life. Moreover, his intellect, unused and untrained, does not possess the versatility and directive power required in the management of machines.

Pauperism seems the only result. Great Britain, the foremost nation in mechanical invention, furnishes in times of war when food is dear aid or entire support for one million and a half of paupers. Of its men, women, and children, one in twenty is a pauper. In the United States, the only rival of Great Britain in productive industry, pauperism is held in check to a greater degree through school education and the facilities for migration to unsettled frontiers.

Face to face with this great question of readjustment of vocations, stands this other great social question of the determination of vocation by the distinction of sex.

The transition of civilization from the standpoint of thralldom to that of freedom has been rendered possible through the great movement in productive industry just discussed. The immense increase of production in the comforts and necessities of life—food, clothing, and shelter—has lifted man above squalor and drudgery to satisfy the pangs of hunger and cold. Increasing leisure has been given for the culture of his mind and spiritual faculties. In consequence of this, the lower and lowest strata of society have risen in the scale of educated intelligence. Their law-obeying and their law-making powers have increased, and they have demanded and received a representation in the government.

The distinction of sex, as we have seen, availed

during the epoch of the division of labor to confine the sphere of woman to the family and to give man the province of productive industry. Persistency is the type in the field of the division of labor. Periodicity is the type of labor in the family. Repetition of the same thing, concentration upon one thing, is the characteristic of labor in the industries. Diversity and versatility are the characteristics of the labor in the family; engaged this hour in preparing the breakfast and washing the dishes; the next making the beds and sweeping the rooms; the next cleansing and mending the clothing; the next knitting or weaving; the next, and at intervals during the whole day, attending to the myriad wants of childhood.

The labor within the family does not admit of division of labor, although it is diversified and in need of such division. The woman prepared for the life of the family, therefore, needed an education which gave her versatility, while the man needed a training for concentration upon one thing.

Persistency and periodicity have, therefore, been said to characterize respectively the spheres of labor of men and women. Within the family endless change from one occupation to one totally different, while in the arts and trades, the sphere of men, there has reigned persistence and mechanical concentration of will power. Before the era of division of labor there was an entirely different condition of things. In the savage state, as above shown, when the tribal form of government prevailed and the center of a state or tribal jurisdiction was at the most a day's march from a hostile frontier, man gave his whole attention to defense and had no strength left for productive industry. He faced a hostile power, uncertain and indefinite, and was obliged to be constantly on the alert. He dissipated his force and utterly unfitted himself for dealing with definite or routine tasks and prescribed duties. To woman belonged then not only the function of family nurture, but also the business of providing food, clothing, and shelter—the sphere of productive industry. Hunting was training for war, and too intermittent and dependent upon caprice to rank as a vocation. It would seem from this, that in the savage state of society woman has the part of providing for what is routine and requires persistence; while man develops solely versatility in the form of cunning and intermittent effort. In primeval society, woman, assisted by children and superannuated men, performs the labor of the family and civil society. In the first epoch of productive industry she limits herself to the sphere of the family more and more.

In the epoch of labor-saving machines the characteristic mental faculty of versatility that belongs to woman creates a louder and louder call for her entrance upon the sphere of productive industry. Not physical force but alertness of intellect being needed in the industries, woman is preferred for managing the power loom and the making of Waltham watches. In the last and highest period of industrial development, the distinction between the spheres of the family and civil society or productive industry is removed. Woman needs and receives an education in the sciences and arts and accomplishments necessary to man. Besides this, the labor-saving machine takes up and performs one after the other each of the special industries that formerly belonged to the family, and thus emancipates woman from drudgery. Weaving, knitting, and sewing have, for the most part, been left to labor-saving machinery; the other occupations in the preparation of food and clothing are rapidly taking the same course. The school, itself, already become a vocation established for the relief of the family, extends its ministrations through the kindergarten and such instrumentalities for the further relief of the family.

The strictly educational influence of the family is called nurture. Parental care watches over the years of helplessness and slowly trains childhood into the forms and conventionalities of civilized life. The general characteristic of nurture is the fact that physical and intellectual maturity devotes itself to the wants and capacities of helpless infancy, and with infinite patience draws out and encourages self-development and free activity in the child. The treatment due to the mature man or woman would destroy the child. The fact that the special vocation of woman, in so far as determined by sex, involves this special feature of nurture furnishes us a significant point to be considered in the discussion of this theme. It indicates that, as government comes to be less a matter of abstract justice and more a matter of providing for the people that which will enhance their capacity for self-activity, woman's aid will be more and more needed in political affairs. Education is one of the functions that appertains to this providing for what will further the self-activity of its citizens. All of the weaklings of the community need more or less to have nurture provided for them in the shape of educational and other restraining and directing influences. Woman is by nature adapted to this work, and will find a very important field of activity in this phase of municipal administration.

From these considerations of the trend of social evolution we are led to see that the equal education of woman with man is certain to prevail in the future.

The age is an age of directive power rather than of drudgery, and directive power requires not mere persistency but also versatility.

In this series of educational works we print this somewhat special work of Miss Helene Lange on the higher education of women in Europe because of its interest to English-speaking nations which have advanced beyond the first steps and engaged actively in establishing institutions of various character for the higher education of women. In this polemical work, written for the most conservative people in Europe in this matter of female education, we may behold reflected as in a mirror the entire movement in all countries, and see all of its stages, from the initiation on to the most advanced line of progress, in one picture.

Dr. Klemm, the translator, has completed the survey of the entire field by his admirable conspectuses in his introduction.

W. T. HARRIS.

WASHINGTON, D. C., *October, 1890.*

CONTENTS.

	PAGE
Editor's Preface	v
Introduction by the Translator	xxi
Chart I. Ratio of Female Teachers in Elementary Schools	xxiii
" II. Ratio of Female Students in Universities	xxiv
" III. Ratio of Girls in Secondary Schools	xxv
" IV. Ratio of Mixed Schools (Coeducation)	xxvi
List of Colleges and Universities for Women	xxix
" Other Institutions for the Superior Instruction of Women	xxix
" Annexes to Male Colleges and Universities	xxxiii
" Colleges and Universities for Both Sexes	xxxiii
Miss H. Lange's Views on Female Education. Introduction	1

CHAPTER

I. Early Movement in England	7
II. First Female Colleges in England	24
III. Women and the Medical Profession	42
IV. Female Secondary Schools in England	61
V. Moral Education in England and Germany	81
VI. Intellectual Education in England and Germany	98
VII. In Other Countries of Europe	110
VIII. Why Women should be admitted to Universities	120
IX. Cause of the Failure in Germany. (*a*) Adverse Circumstances; (*b*) Man's Unwillingness to aid the Cause; (*c*) Woman's Indifference	146

INTRODUCTION BY THE TRANSLATOR.

THE question of higher female education is not new in this country, and to some it may seem as though it had lost the character of a problem with us. While it is true that nowhere on the face of the earth woman occupies so elevated a position as here; that nowhere is her inborn right to education more readily and willingly acknowledged than here; that nowhere are more schools, colleges, and universities open to woman than here; that nowhere has woman found so many chances for employment in consequence of liberal provisions for her education; and that nowhere has the maxim of Diesterweg, "Education is liberation," been proved more conclusively than here, it can not be said that the facts concerning woman's higher education are as well known as is desirable. This is shown by the numerous inquiries sent to the Bureau of Education, in Washington, concerning the progress made in this and other countries. To many who know that America has taken the lead in this question, it would seem superfluous to learn what European nations think and do in regard to it; but the frequency of the inquiries prove an ever growing interest in the matter. Aside from the fact that it is always interesting to see what others do, it should be borne in mind that our almost insular seclusion from the European world of thought and action is likely to make us exclusive. Hence it may prove instructive to learn how the question, which with us seems nearly solved, is agitating the minds of European educators and legislators. Casting about for suitable material to submit to American readers, the translator came into possession of a little book written by Miss Helene Lange* which is so characteristic an *exposé* of the question mentioned, and combines with a historic review and vigorous arguments so many valuable statements concerning the actual facts in England, France, Germany, and other countries, that he concluded to render it in English without alterations and omissions or additions. It may seem as though the work of Helene Lange is only the expression of one side, but the frequent mention of men well known as educational authorities and her liberal quotations from male writers save her from the accusation of partiality. Hence we may safely " submit the case to the jury." The accompanying statistical charts (I to IV) are offered with some degree of confidence that they will meet the demand of the numerous inquiries. A few explanations seem necessary, hence they follow each chart.

---

* Frauenbildung, by Helene Lange. Berlin, 1889. L. Oehmigke's Verlag.

Chart I.
RATIO OF FEMALE TEACHERS
TO WHOLE NUMBER OF TEACHERS EMPLOYED.

IN THE UNITED STATES, IN 1886.	63% WOMEN.	37% MEN.
IN THE CITIES OF THE UNITED STATES, IN 1888.	90.4% WOMEN.	9.6% MEN.
IN ENGLAND, IN 1888.	69% WOMEN.	31% MEN.
IN FRANCE, IN 1888.	54.5% WOMEN.	45.5% MEN.
IN PRUSSIA, †) IN 1887.	10.6% WOMEN.	89.4% MEN.
IN AUSTRIA, IN 1887.	22.7% WOMEN.	77.3% MEN.
IN SWITZERLAND, IN 1887.	32% WOMEN.	68% MEN.
IN ITALY, IN 1887.	53% WOMEN.	47% MEN.

†). THE RATIO OF WOMEN IS ESTIMATED TO BE 15.7% IN 1888.

This chart shows the *Ratio of Female Teachers* to the whole number of teachers employed in the public schools of this country: (a) *for the whole country;* (b) *for the cities only.**

The ratio for England was found by taking the number of female teachers, assistants, and pupil teachers in all the schools of England and Wales receiving state aid (see official report for 1888). This includes only elementary schools. Hence it does not, as in the ratio for our country, include high schools and other secondary schools. The ratio for France was found by footing up the reports of the different department inspectors of France. This was done in preference to using the annual report of the Minister of Education for 1886, in order to obtain a more recent statement of facts. The ratio of female teachers in Prussia was obtained from the official report of 1887, the latest information obtainable. The same is to be said of Austria, Switzerland, and Italy.

In order to facilitate the comparison offered, the year of which the statistics were taken is stated in each case.

---

* See Annual Report of the Commissioner of Education for 1887-'88, pp. 75 and 390.

Chart II.
RATIO OF FEMALE STUDENTS
TO WHOLE NUMBER OF STUDENTS PURSUING SUPERIOR EDUCATION IN UNIVERSITIES AND COLLEGES.

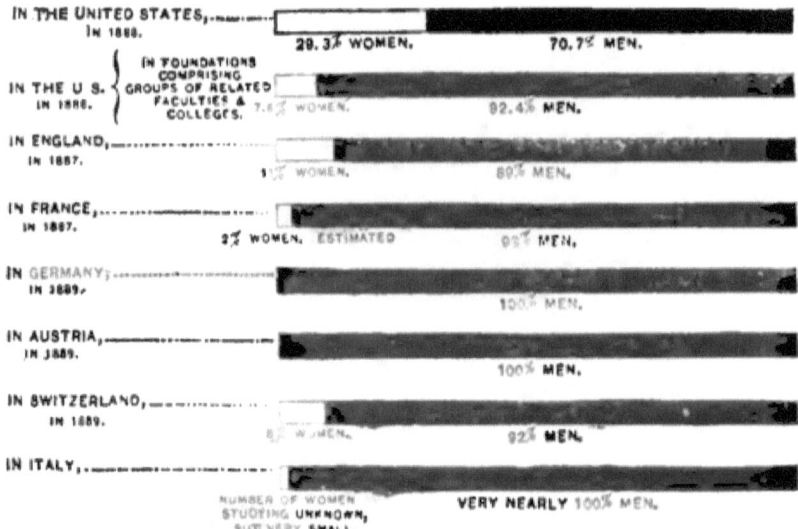

The *Ratio of Female Students* to the whole number of students pursuing superior education (university and college students) for the United States is given (1) For the whole country (excluding all preparatory departments); (2) For institutions comprising groups of related faculties and colleges. (See Annual Report of the Commissioner of Education for 1887-'88, pp. 582 and 624.) For England an estimate of Miss H. Lange (see p. 65 of this book) is used; no definite statement has ever been published. For France, the official reports do not give the desired information, hence an estimate is given which is based on information contained in The Woman Question, by Theodore Stanton. In Prussia, the annual reports mention no female students. None are matriculated, hence no degrees are conferred upon women. In Austria, women are permitted to attend some lectures, but they are considered private students; they are prohibited from matriculation and graduation. Full and accurate information concerning Switzerland was obtained from the excellent Jahrbuch, of Grob, for 1887-'88. The ratio given for Italy is based on estimates derived from sundry sources, chiefly educational journals.

Chart III.
RATIO OF GIRLS
IN HIGH AND OTHER SECONDARY SCHOOLS.

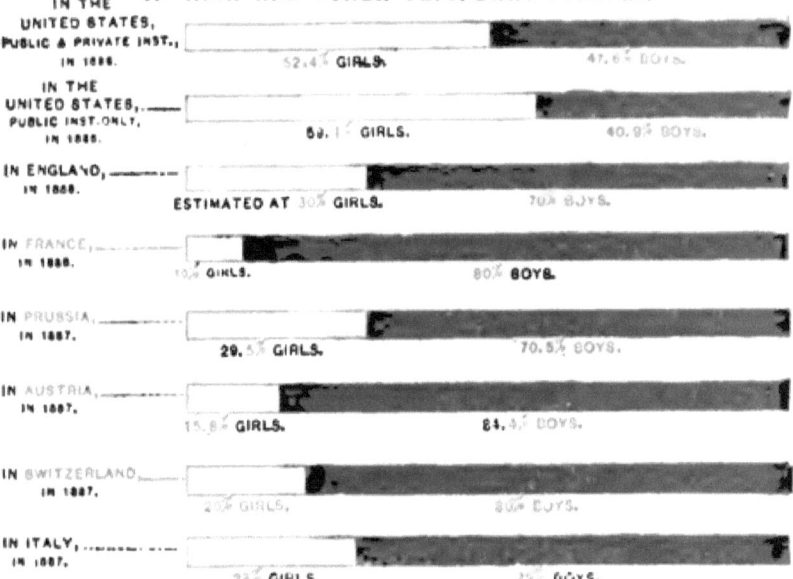

The *Ratio of Girls* in high schools or other secondary schools given for the United States is taken from the Annual Report of the Commissioner of Education for 1887–'88. It is given (1) for all institutions, public and private schools; (2) for public schools alone. In both cases it exceeds that of the boys. For England it is impossible to obtain a correct statement in regard to the number of pupils in secondary schools, owing to the fact that these schools are not under governmental supervision, hence the ratio given in this chart is to be taken "*cum grano salis.*" It was based upon statements of Miss Lange, The Educational Times (London), Sir Lyon Playfair, and others. For France, Prussia, Austria, Switzerland, and Italy, official statements were available. It must be taken into consideration, however, in order to arrive at a proper estimate of the ratios in this chart, that many institutions in this country classed among the secondary schools are little if anything more than elementary schools; hence it is safe to think that the ratio given for the United States is somewhat exaggerated.

Chart IV.
RATIO OF MIXED SCHOOLS
(CONTAINING BOTH BOYS AND GIRLS)
OF THE TOTAL NUMBER OF ELEMENTARY SCHOOLS.

IN THE UNITED STATES, IN 1866. — 86% MIXED SCHOOLS, (ONLY AN ESTIMATE). GIRLS. BOYS.

IN THE UNITED STATES, IN 1885. — THE NORMAL SCHOOLS HAVE 72.6% FEMALE STUDENTS AND 27.4% MALE STU.

IN ENGLAND, IN 1887. — 68% MIXED SCHOOLS. 15.3% GIRLS. 16.7% BOYS.

IN FRANCE, IN 1887. — 24.1% MIXED. 41.7% GIRLS' SCHOOLS. 34.2% BOYS' SCHOOLS.

IN PRUSSIA, IN 1887. — 73% MIXED SCHOOLS. 13.6% GIRLS. 13.4% BOYS.

IN AUSTRIA, IN 1887. — 87.8% MIXED SCHOOLS. 5.3% 6.9% GIRLS. BOYS.

IN SWITZERLAND, IN 1887. — 85% MIXED SCHOOLS. GIRLS.

IN ITALY, IN 1887. — 16.3% MIXED. 32.9% GIRLS' SCHOOLS. 41.8% BOYS' SCHOOLS.

This chart is intended to show what extent *co-education of the sexes* has found. The ratios of mixed schools (schools in which both sexes are taught in the same rooms) are those for elementary schools only, except for the United States, where the public high schools are included. For this country, however, only an estimate could be given, based on information published by the Bureau of Education in 1883 (Co-education of the Sexes, Circular of Information, No. 2). The most diligent research among the statistical material on hand has not sufficed to arrive at an accurate statement. The same may be said of England. But the official reports of France, Prussia, Italy, and Austria were very explicit and accurate concerning this point. For Switzerland, the Jahrbuch of Grob (1887) furnished the necessary information.

It may be stated here that the statistics of Prussia may be taken as a standard of measurement for Germany. The differences between Prussia and the other states of Germany are not great enough to materially alter the ratios given in the foregoing four charts.

After this general and graphic presentation of statistical facts, it seems desirable to state briefly the facilities offered in this country for the higher education of women. If this were but to show the great difference existing between the Old and the New World in the appreciation of the right of woman to higher education, the end would justify the space occupied. But it is chiefly done to prove that in this country the woman question as relating to education is scarcely a problem any longer. We must for obvious reasons refrain from entering into historical statements; that would necessitate lengthy biographical presentations of the lives and public efforts of several noble women, such as Mrs. Emma Willard, Miss Catherine E. Beecher, Mary Lyon, Miss Grant, and others. That, of course, is out of the question. The reader is kindly referred to Theodore Stanton's book The Woman Question and to vol. xi of this series, Boone's Education in the United States (page 362 to the end), which books contain many valuable details.

The latest report of the United States Commissioner of Education (that of 1887–'88) groups under the head of "superior instruction" all institutions the intent and purport of which is an academic and professional education (except the normal schools), and states the sum total of these institutions to be 988, the number of their professors 12,409, and the number of their students 145,446, itemized as follows:

	No. of schools.	No. of professors.	No. of students.
Universities and colleges of arts and sciences..................	357	4,834	75,333
Colleges and seminaries for women.	207	2,581	25,318
Colleges endowed with the national land grant..................	32	620	8,127
Schools of science not so endowed..	30	348	7,976
Schools of theology..............	138	726	6,512
Schools of law...................	49	293	3,667
Schools of medicine, dentistry, etc..	175	3,007	18,513
Totals..................	988	12,409	145,446

Provision for the higher education of women is made (*a*) in colleges and seminaries exclusively for women, and (*b*) in co-education colleges. The entire attendance of young women in the several classes of institutions for 1887-'88, so far as reported, was as follows:

	No. of students.	
Colleges and seminaries for women.	25,318	⎫ = 29% of the number of students in superior institutions.
Colleges of arts and sciences......	16,428	
Colleges of agriculture and the mechanic arts endowed with the national land grant............	917	⎭
Total.....................	42,663	

Of 357 colleges of liberal arts, 217 admit women; of 32 independent colleges endowed with the national land grant, 20 report students of both sexes. This gives a total of 237 co-education colleges. Later reports may show still larger numbers.

Nothing seems more conclusive than a perusal of the following lists, of which it may be expressly stated that the number of students mentioned is that

INTRODUCTION BY THE TRANSLATOR. xxix

of the collegiate departments, and does not include the students in the preparatory departments.

I. COLLEGES AND UNIVERSITIES FOR WOMEN.

(Institutions marked thus * have a female president.)

NAME AND LOCATION.	Male professors	Female professors	No. of students	Date of opening	No. of degrees conferred
Smith College, Northampton, Mass.*	11	13	312	1875	54
Wellesley College, Wellesley, Mass.*	7	70	628	1875	62
Wells College, Aurora, N. Y.	15		28	1868	
Elmira College, Elmira, N. Y.	14		81		
Ingham University, Le Roy, N. Y.	2	15	59	1835	
Rutgers Female College, New York, N. Y.	11		37		
Vassar College, Poughkeepsie, N. Y.	6	28	299	1865	36
Bryn Mawr College, Bryn Mawr, Pa.	14	5	84	1885	2
Mt. Holyoke College, South Hadley, Mass.*	5	25	314	1837	

"This table includes a group of institutions whose admission requirements, standards of instruction, and general organization accord with those that have long been characteristic of colleges of liberal arts. Their work is essentially collegiate, in which respect they differ from the older seminaries for women, which, while making more or less provision for the distinctive studies of the college curriculum, are schools for general instruction." (Report of Commissioner of Education for 1887-'88.)

II. INSTITUTIONS FOR THE SUPERIOR INSTRUCTION OF WOMEN.

(Those marked with an * have a female president or principal.)

In *Alabama*: Athens Female College, Union Female College, Huntsville Female College, Huntsville Female Seminary, Judson Female Institute, Marion Female Seminary, Synodical Female Institute, Central Female College, Tuskaloosa Female College, Alabama Conference Female College. Total number of students: 543.

In *California*: The Ellis College, Mills College, Santa Rosa Ladies' College. Total number of students: 350.

xxx HIGHER EDUCATION OF WOMEN IN EUROPE.

In *Connecticut*: Hartford Female Seminary.* Number of students: 50.

In *Georgia*: Lucy Cobb Institute,* Methodist Female College, Andrew Female College, Dalton Female College, Monroe Female College, Baptist Seminary for Young Ladies, Griffin Female College, La Grange Female College, Southern Female College, Wesleyan Female College, College Temple, Shorter College, Young Female College. Total number of students: 1,055.

In *Illinois*: Seminary of the Sacred Heart.* Almira College, Illinois Female College, Jacksonville Female Academy, St. Mary's School, Chicago Female College, Mt. Carroll Seminary,* Rockford Seminary.* Total number of students: 488.

In *Indiana*: De Pauw College for Young Women. Number of students: 31.

In *Iowa*: Immaculate Conception Academy,* Callahan College. Total number of students: 149.

In *Kansas*: College for Young Ladies,* College of the Sisters of Bethany. Total number of students: 147.

In *Kentucky*: Caldwell College,* Georgetown Female Seminary, Liberty Female College, Daughters' College, Bethel Female College, Hamilton Female College, St. Catherine's Female Academy,* Sayre Female Institute, Hampton College, Louisville Female College, Millersburg Female College, Mt. Sterling Female College, Jessamine Female Institute,* Kentucky College for Young Ladies, Logan Female College, Science Hill School, Stuart's Female College, Stanford Female College, Cedar Bluff Female College. Total number of students: 1,127.

In *Louisiana*: Silliman Female Collegiate Institute, Mansfield Female College. Total number of students: 126.

In *Maine*: Westbrook Seminary and Female College, Wesleyan Seminary and Female College. Total number of students: 255.

In *Maryland*: Baltimore Academy of the Visitation,* Baltimore Female College, Cambridge Female Seminary, Frederick Female Seminary, Lutherville Seminary. Total number of students: 363.

In *Massachusetts*: Abbot Academy, Lasell Seminary for Young Women, Gannett Institute, Bradford Academy,* Wheaton Female Seminary. Total number of students: 848.

INTRODUCTION BY THE TRANSLATOR. xxxi

In *Michigan*: Michigan Female Seminary.* Number of students: 41.

In *Minnesota*: Albert Lea College, St. Mary's Hall,* Bennett Seminary.* Total number of students: 229.

In *Mississippi*: Blue Mountain Female College, Whitworth Female College, Central Female Institute, College for the Education of White Girls, Corinth Female College,* Franklin Female College,* East Mississippi Female College, Union Female College, Chickasaw Female College, Port Gibson Female College, Shuqualak Female College, Starkville Female Institute, Lea Female College. Total number of students: 954.

In *Missouri*: Christian Female College, Stephens Female College, Howard Female College, Fulton Synodical Female College, Woodland College, St. Louis Seminary, Baptist Female College, Central Female College, Elizabeth Aull Female Seminary, Hardin College, Lindenwood Female College, Mary Institute, Ursuline Academy.* Total number of students: 1,228.

In *Nevada*: Bishop Whitaker's School for Girls. Number of students: 73.

In *New Hampshire*: Robinson Female Seminary, Conference Seminary and Female College, Tilden Seminary. Total number of students: 348.

In *New Jersey*: Bordentown Female College, St. Mary's Hall,* Freehold Young Ladies' Seminary.* Total number of students: 113.

In *New York*: Academies of the Sacred Heart (3),* St. Agnes School,* Brooklyn Heights Seminary, Packer Collegiate Institute, Buffalo Female Academy, Granger Place School,* Academy of Mount St. Vincent,* Boarding and Day Schools for Young Ladies (2),* D'Youville Academy.* Total number of students: 1,740.

In *North Carolina*: Asheville Female College, Charlotte Female Institute, Greensborough Female College, Davenport Female College, Baptist Female Institute, Wesleyan Female College, Oxford Female Seminary, Estey Seminary, Peace Institute, St. Mary's School, Statesville Female College.* Thomasville Female College. Total number of students: 950.

In *Ohio*: Bartholomew English and Classical School, Cincinnati Wesleyan College, Mt. Auburn Young Ladies' Institute,

Glendale Female College, Granville Female College, Shepardson College,* Hillsborough Female College, Oxford Female College, Western Female Seminary,* Lake Erie Female Seminary.* Total number of students: 823.

In *Oregon*: St. Helen's Hall.* Number of students: 132.

In *Pennsylvania*: Allentown Female College, Moravian Seminary, Blairsville Ladies' Seminary, Wilson College, Boarding and Day School,* Brooke Hall Female Seminary, Ogontz School for Young Ladies,* Philadelphia Seminary,* Pittsburg Female College, Washington Female Seminary.* Total number of students: 823.

In *South Carolina*: Columbia Female College, Due West Female College,* Greenville Female College, Walhalla Female College. Total number of students: 410.

In *Tennessee*: Brownsville Female College, Wesleyan Female College, Columbian Athenæum, Conference Female Institute, Cumberland Female College, Soule Female College, Nashville College for Young Ladies, St. Cecilia Academy,* Seminary for Young Ladies, Martin Female College, Synodical Female College,* Shelbyville Female College, Mary Sharp College. Total number of students: 860.

In *Texas*: Baylor Female College, Nazareth Academy,* Waco Female College. Total number of students: 328.

In *Vermont*: Methodist Female College. Number of students: 84.

In *Virginia*: Martha Washington College, Albemarle Female Institute, Montgomery Female College,* Danville College for Young Ladies, Roanoke Female College, Hollin's Institute, Marion Female College, Norfolk College for Young Ladies, Southern Female College, Staunton Female Seminary, Virginia Female Institute,* Wesleyan Female Institute, Fauquier Institute, Valley Female College. Total number of students: 727.

In *West Virginia*: Broaddus College, Parkersburg Female Seminary,* Wheeling Female College. Total number of students: 110.

In *Wisconsin*: Wisconsin Female College,* Milwaukee College, St. Clara Academy.* Total number of students: 127.

INTRODUCTION BY THE TRANSLATOR. xxxiii

III. Annexes to Male Colleges and Universities.

Harvard University Annex, Cambridge, Mass., 103 female students; Columbia College Annex, New York, N. Y., 28 female students; Ladies' Annex, Southwestern University, Georgetown, Texas, 89 female students.

IV. Colleges and Universities for Both Sexes.

A. Foundations comprising Groups of Related Faculties.

Columbian University, Washington, D. C., 34 female students; De Pauw University, Greencastle, Ind., 260 female students; Boston University, Boston, Mass., 256 female students; Cornell University, Ithaca, N. Y., 139 female students.

B. State Universities open to Both Sexes.

(The numbers in parentheses state the number of female pupils in 1887-'88.)

The State universities of California (54), Colorado (16), Illinois (58), Indiana (69), Iowa (86), Kansas (55), Michigan (191), Minnesota (95), Mississippi (6), Missouri (100), Nebraska (73), Nevada (37), Ohio (28), Oregon (9), Texas (42), Wisconsin (104).

C. Other Colleges and Seminaries open to Women.

(The numbers in parentheses are the number of female students in the State.)

In *Alabama*: Selma University (3).

In *Arkansas*: Cane Hill College, Little Rock University and Philander Smith College (15).

In *California*: Pierce Christian College, University of Southern California, Napa College, University of the Pacific, Pacific Methodist College, San Joaquin College, Hesperian College (224).

In *Colorado*: Colorado College, University of Denver (17).

In *District of Columbia*: Howard University (1).

In *Georgia*: Bowdon College (37).

In *Illinois*: Hedding College, Illinois Wesleyan University, Carthage College, Eureka College, Northwestern University, Ewing College, Northern Illinois College, Knox College, Lombard University, Lake Forest University, McKendree College, Lincoln University, Monmouth College, Northwestern College, Chaddock College, Augustana College, Shurtleff College, Westfield College, Wheaton College (481).

In *Indiana*: Franklin College, Hanover College, Hartsville College, Butler University, Morris Hill College, Earlham College (162).

In *Iowa*: Amity College, Griswold College, Drake University, University of Des Moines, Parsons College, Upper Iowa University, Iowa College, Lenox College, Simpson College, German College, Cornell College, Oskaloosa College, Penn College, Central University of Iowa, Tabor College, Western College (547).

In *Kansas*: Baker University, College of Emporia, Highland University, Campbell University, Ottawa University, Kansas Wesleyan University, Washburn College, Garfield University (156).

In *Kentucky*: Berea College, Eminence College, South Kentucky College, Murray Institute (240).

In *Louisiana*: Keachie College, New Orleans University, Straight University, Tulane University (100).

In *Maine*: Bates College, Colby University (54).

In *Maryland*: Windsor College, West Maryland College (77).

In *Michigan*: Albion College, Hillsdale College, Hope College, Kalamazoo College, Olivet College (151).

In *Minnesota*: Hamlin University, Carleton College (63).

In *Mississippi*: Kavanaugh College (60).

In *Missouri*: Pike County College, Lewis College, Pritchett Institute, Morrisville College, Washington University, Drury College, Tarkio College, Central Wesleyan College, Mary Institute, Washington University (289).

In *Montana*: College of Montana (14).

In *Nebraska*: Nebraska Central College, Doane College, Gates College (126).

In *New Mexico*: University of New Mexico (50).

In *New York*: St. Lawrence University, Syracuse University (195).

In *North Carolina*: Rutherford College, Livingston College, Weaverville College, Shaw University (81).

In *Ohio*: Buchtel College, Ohio University, Baldwin University, German Wallace College, Calvin College, University of Cincinnati, Adelbert College, Belmont College, Ohio Wesleyan

University, Findlay College, Twin Valley College, Denison University, Hiram College, Mt. Union College, Muskingum College, Oberlin College, Rio Grande College, Scio College, Wittenberg College, Heidelberg College, Urbana University, Otterbein University, Wilmington College, University of Wooster, Antioch College (1,039).

In *Oregon*: Pacific University, McMinnville College, Willamette University (18).

In *Pennsylvania*: Lebanon Valley College, Geneva College, Dickinson College, Ursinus College, Thiel College, Grove City College, Bucknell University, Allegheny College, Central Pennsylvania College, Westminter College, University of Pennsylvania, Swarthmore College (328).

In *Tennessee*: Grant Memorial University, Chattanooga University, Bethel College, Maryville College, Milligan College, Central Tennessee College, Fisk University, Greenville and Tusculum College (72).

In *Texas*: Wesleyan College, Salado College, Trinity University, Baylor University (157).

In *Vermont*: University of Vermont, Middlebury College (25).

In *Washington*: University of Washington, Whitman College (28).

In *West Virginia*: West Virginia College (1).

In *Wisconsin*: Lawrence University, Galesville University, Milton College, Ripon College (82).

It is probable that among the names of institutions for higher education in the foregoing lists there are not a few that can not well be classed with universities and colleges as these terms are understood in Europe, but the writer has no means of ascertaining their rank or standing. Even if all such schools are eliminated from the list, the number of those who deserve to remain in it would be most gratifying to any one who firmly believes in woman's higher education. If there be any one who does not, the foregoing pages may supply information which is adapted to change his mind. It is sincerely hoped that the showing made on the comparative charts will aid the cause here and abroad.

L. R. KLEMM.

WASHINGTON, D. C., *September, 1890.*

HIGHER EDUCATION OF WOMEN IN EUROPE.

INTRODUCTION.

It is one of the symptoms of our time that all important journals and magazines open their columns for discussions of the "woman question"; that innumerable pamphlets, yes, even voluminous books, are written to bring it nearer a solution. In all civilized nations it approaches a solution, and lately we frequently meet, in foreign and home journals, the statement that the German is the only and last great nation of culture which leaves its women under the oppression of middle-age fetters, keeping closed against them the institutions of higher learning—that is, the requisites of every higher professional activity, and thus effectually preventing the solution of the burning question, which is only possible through intellectual emancipation. The absurdity of these conditions is correctly stated by Mrs. Kettler when she says: "The education of to-day retains woman in a state of minority or tutelage. . . . A child is a minor, hence it is supported. The woman is also regarded as a minor—hence she must support herself. The child is asked: Are you hungry? Here is bread; eat. The woman is told: If you are hungry, earn your bread. See, up yonder are many loaves; if you reach them, you may eat as many as you like; but mind, don't use that ladder to get at them—that's made for men. Perhaps a loaf will fall ere long; only have patience. Perhaps they'll come down by themselves; only be patient." *

What is the reason the German woman can not obtain what the woman of other civilized nations obtained? Is the reason to be looked for in themselves? Or in the men? Or in insurmountable exterior obstacles? Much depends upon the answer to this question; for it is decisive in the choice of roads to be traveled. A study of the development of the woman question in other nations perhaps will give us a clew. Kindred England seems best suited to such consideration and study. It will be necessary to determine in what regard the movement now so happily terminated is typical; while the specialties traceable to national peculiarities and obvious in

---

* Woman's Profession, by Mrs. Kettler, vol. ii, p. 16, January, 1888.

specifically English institutions must not be made subjects of imitation. But that which the *English women* have accomplished recedes behind that which *women* have accomplished; the national must give precedence to the international; for the woman question *is* an international problem. Common interests of culture unite the women *of all countries*, and it is a beautiful feature of the movement yet so young that there exists between the women of different, and even antagonistic, nations, a mutual appreciation not always found among men. That is the reason why we women are apt to learn of and from each other.

I will preface my essay by stating that I have been warned not to make public what these pages contain. In the first place, it is argued that this is not a time favorable to women; second, it is apprehended that a cause which may boast of having succeeded in England is likely to be discredited in Germany. I answer, 1, that I can not see how the time can become more favorable for the women by patient waiting and ominous silence; 2, that the prejudices of the multitude and non-thinking people—if at all it should be admitted that truth must be treated diplomatically — possibly might come into consideration if I had to deal with the multitude; but that is far from being the case.

The present book is offered to the thinking men and women of the nation; hence the apprehensions mentioned are superfluous. I therefore enter upon my subject without further prefatory remarks.

About the present English girl's and woman's education there are many erroneous opinions in vogue in Germany. We have perhaps given less attention during the last twenty years to the educational efforts of foreign nations than they deserve, and the reforms effected there seem to have become known scarcely to the narrowest professional circles. Thus we hear the English female education again and again denounced as below par. That is owing to some obvious causes. Twenty years ago, for instance, the harshest criticism of the English girls' schools was fully justified; they simply could not be worse. He who was in England previous to 1868 could not help but come to that conclusion. Now, knowing how an opinion once generally adopted remains unchanged, even long after it has lost its basis of fact, it is not to be wondered at that even to this day, in Germany, the people should think so little of English female education.

Again, the experiences made here and there with English girls in German boarding schools seem to

have given weight to the generally accepted opinion
or prejudice. That seems an argument of little
weight. It is well known that a people can only be
studied in its own native country, never in foreign
countries, where, through want of familiarity with
the language and customs, it is at a disadvantage.
In this particular case there are other considerations.
1. The education of English young girls is throughout different in quality from that of German young
ladies. They possibly have knowledge in ancient
languages and mathematics, which with us is not
considered a female accomplishment, while they are
deficient in modern languages, literature, and history, and hence rarely fit into a school with an
orthodox course of study. 2. Moreover, by far the
greatest number of young English women frequent-
ing German boarding schools come from social
strata that educate their girls by private governesses.
Hence an apparent want of knowledge in these few
pupils should not permit us to argue from them
upon others, or all others; and we should certainly
not reject English higher education on account of
the few specimens whom we are hardly able to
judge.

It is a fact, at any rate, that girls' education, and,
indeed, the entire female education in England has
been subjected to a change so radical that it can

scarcely be conceived. The most interesting part of it is the manner in which this change was brought about. The following chapters may attempt to show that.

CHAPTER I.

EARLY MOVEMENT IN ENGLAND.

THE first traces of the woman's movement in England may be found as early as the last century. In 1792 Mary Wollstonecraft published her Vindication of the Rights of Women; during our century Sydney Smith, and above all, John Stuart Mill, with the sharpest of intellectual weapons, continued their energetic attempts in assisting woman in the acquisition of her rights—rights that had been suppressed since the beginning of the world. The political side of the movement shall not here be touched. Toward the middle of this century the attempt was made to give woman a share of the highest culture of her time, and to enable her to contribute to its elevation and extension. It was a beginning of a *social* revolution at the time when Europe was convulsed with the throes of *political* revolution. People began to see that the culture of woman means the culture of the people. Hence influential persons tried to elevate the education of girls, and since it is but logical that if the schools should be improved the teachers must first be improved—that is, receive the proper professional preparation—it was decided to begin with the establishment of institutions which would give adult women and girls beyond school age a thorough professional education. The first of these institutions, *Queen's College*, in London, was established in 1848, with special intention to prepare female teachers and governesses. The college owes its existence especially to some professors of King's College, among whom were Rev. C. G. Nicolay and Rev. F. D. Maurice. Since the previous school education of the students of Queen's College was found frequently quite insufficient, preparatory classes were added. Soon the college courses could be extended. They embrace to-day Religion and Church History, Elementary and Higher Mathematics, Latin, Greek, Modern Languages, History, Natural Sciences, Logic, Ethics, and Music.

Queen's College will always be of great interest, being the oldest of the English female colleges; but it is not the type of the present English colleges.*

---

* The term college is often applied in England to what in continental Europe is considered a secondary *school*, the course of which is higher than that of an elementary or grammar school. In the strictest acceptation of the word it means a building (attached to an English university) in which the students live together. Since a great part of the studying is

It has, till the present day, retained the character it received at its foundation. It is the only female college managed by men. It follows, with the best of intentions, a careful system of adaptation in presenting the matter of instruction to its students, which is not compatible with strict science. But since the intention is not made secret but stated plainly, and publicly at that, no objection can be raised.* The college accomplishes one great object; like the courses which have recently been opened to the women in King's College, in London, it offers educated, but non-professional persons a chance for continuing their studies, and hence resembles in that our Victoria-Lyceum (in Berlin).

A second institution soon followed. During the same year (1848) a Miss Reid, in London, was "surprised" by the receipt of a letter containing the information that half a dozen honorable gentlemen, at a friendly banquet, had discussed the unsatisfactory state of female education, and concluded to

---

done in these students' dwellings, the name has in due course of time been transferred to other institutions which offer higher education, notably those which prepare for the university examinations, though no boarding and lodging establishment is connected with them.

* "The college does not undertake to provide the full instruction which may be required for the degree examinations of the University of London." Queen's College Calendar, 1888, p. 35.

do something to alleviate the wrong done to the female sex, since they could not consider it right that the many benevolent and charitable institutions established for the education of the *youth* of the country should be utilized exclusively by boys and young men.

The half-dozen honorable men, and, in fact, the whole letter, proved to be a pious deception of Miss Reid, who in this way thought to introduce to the public a plan which lay nearest her heart. She had aided zealously in founding Queen's College, having herself felt acutely the want of higher intellectual education, and now intended to establish a second college for women in another part of the city, which, indeed, in 1849, was opened under the name of *Bedford College* after surmounting great obstacles.

Bedford College also is still in existence, and has the satisfaction of looking back upon a blessed time of work. Many thoroughly and highly educated women who have devoted their entire lives to the cause of their sex, and served it well, were here educated. At first it was shaped after Queen's College, but later experienced many changes dictated by the spirit of the time; so that at present it is a boarding school (properly speaking), and prepares students for other colleges, and even for the examinations of the University of London.

After this a longer pause is noticed, for not until after 1862 was the miserable condition of female education brought to the notice of the public and the question again agitated. It became evident that more—much more—must be done for the education of young ladies and adults (that only women should conduct the institutions for women was never doubted) if the lower schools should be improved; but the higher education of adults found the most formidable difficulty in the want of proper preparation of the students in the lower schools. Thus the movement was that of a circle, from which an exit has at last been found by artificially inducing the lower schools to increased exertion and care. It is done by introducing a system of official examinations.

For many years the so-called junior and senior examinations had existed for boys, examinations at the ages of fourteen and sixteen respectively, which served to prove the existence of a certain amount of knowledge desirable at these ages. In 1862 a committee was formed which attempted to induce the authorities to admit girls to these examinations. In 1863 a trial examination was held for girls, which had very poor results; but this only gave a fresh impetus to the workers in the cause, and it is specially owing to the exertions of Miss Emily Davies that in

1865 the local examinations were offered to young ladies in Cambridge, and soon afterward in Oxford. Whatever one may think of these examinations, which may in the near future become superfluous, it is not to be denied that they proved of great value for the improvement of female, and particularly girls', education. If they did nothing else, they made it clear that there was much room for improvement.

With an energy without precedent, the English women went to work, and the result is fully commensurate with the efforts made. Within the short space of twenty years, as said before, England has witnessed a complete revolution in female education, aided, as that revolution was, by the fact of its absolute freedom from governmental interference. Of course, higher education of women may miss at times the essential aid which a government could give it if that government understands its time and duties well; but, on the other hand, it will not have to go into the exhausting fight in which many noble combatants perish if the government should be opposed to it.

More and more clearly the women of England recognized that if they wished to bring the movement in favor of higher education for the female sex to a satisfactory conclusion they must not be content with insignificant results—they must have the best the country offers; that, if they should want to keep the higher education of their sex in their own hands and fulfill the important task imposed upon them, they must not shun the exertions which man subjects himself to for the purpose of fulfilling his task—in short, they must aspire to a thorough university education.

A question may be raised as to the correctness of that conclusion. Different tasks, no doubt, are assigned to men and women; numerous physical and psychical differences between them would indicate that, and hence point to the necessity of a difference in intellectual preparation. On the other hand, it is said, There is only *one* science. Certainly. But in the conventional manner of its transmission, in its preparatory studies, in the entire range of universities, there are, according to a common judgment, so many points in which reform is needed that it is pitiable to think that women will have to walk the old worn-out roundabout roads where shorter and much better paved roads might pleasantly lead them to their goal. But, however probable it is that in time to come woman will find, or at least seek, her own ways, it does not admit of doubt, that at present she is not able to do that, being internally not free enough, and that the men would not recognize any other culture as profound and sufficient enough, except one like their own and acquired like their own. This is a truth which we must recognize in Germany. Thus, for instance, experience has by no means proved that the higher professional preparation for teachers, as it is customary with us, is a good preparation *for a teacher of girls;* yet that preparation is thought by these teachers the only correct one. Every proposition to give female teachers for the upper grades a professional training and preparation differing from that given to men, however well adapted it may be, meets among teachers who are known to be friends of the cause with the objection, "That would not be scientific." Though, personally, I consider this objection untenable, and though I believe that one might unhesitatingly use other roads than the customary ones without falling into the error of aiding "half-culture," or adapting science to the so-called female capacities (I can, for instance, not consent to the roundabout way of approaching the sciences through the medium of the ancient languages), yet I can understand that in the nature of the case the women of England first acknowledged the principle: Let women participate in the studies of the men, let them follow the same courses, hence let them pass the same examinations.

How I feel about this personally I shall reveal further on. It must suffice here to state that there were reasons of expediency which influenced the women referred to. They intended to prove that they had the capacity to do what men could do, and thus gain confidence in their own mental faculties. The university courses and the requirements for education were well known—they were current coin. A new course arranged according to woman's views and judgment, even though it might have led to better results, would have found no recognition. This view was represented with special ardor by Miss Davies, who expressed it eloquently in her book (published in 1866) on The Higher Education of Women. The faults and failings of girls' education as hitherto conducted, the necessity of a radical change, the methods to be employed to that end, find a thorough and skillful treatment in the book. Some parts of it may have importance only for English institutions, but most of it is quite applicable to German conditions.

With great earnestness Miss Davies points out the danger lying in the fact that in the age which is most important for the development of character, the years between school and marriage, the girls are left without earnest mental occupation; at best, being induced to occupy themselves with some fancy occupations. What should be done instead? The answer depends upon circumstances. If daughters of the better classes (ladies*), they should receive the education of a lady—the highest, most refined culture of the time.

"The accurate habits of thought and the intellectual polish by which the scholar is distinguished, ought to be no less carefully sought in the training of women than in that of men. This would be true, even if only for the sake of the charm which high culture gives to social intercourse—a charm attainable in no other way. But apart from this consideration, the duties of women of the higher class are such as to demand varied knowledge as well as disciplined mind and character. Difficult cases in social ethics frequently arise on which women are obliged to act and to guide the actions of others. However incompetent they may be, they can not escape the responsibility of judging and deciding. And though natural sagacity and the happy impulses, of which we hear so much, come to their aid, prejudice and mistaken impulses ought also to be taken into the account as disturbing elements of a very misleading kind. In dealing with social difficulties, the

---

* The American reader will kindly bear in mind that Miss Lange writes from the standpoint of the European.

value of a cultivated judgment, able to unravel entangled evidence and to give due weight to a great variety of conflicting considerations, would seem to be obvious enough. It would be well worth while to exchange the wonderful unconscious instinct by which women are supposed to leap to right conclusions, no one knows how, for the conscious power of looking steadily and comprehensively at the whole facts of a case, and thereupon shaping a course of action with a clear conception of its probable issues. Of course, a merely literary education will not give this power. Knowledge of the world and of human nature, only to be gained by observation and experience, go farther than mere knowledge of books. But the habit of impartiality and deliberation—of surveying a wide field of thought—and of penetrating, so far as human eye can see, into the heart of things, which is promoted by genuine study even of books alone, tends to produce an attitude of mind favorable for the consideration of complicated questions of any sort. A comparison between the judgment of a scholar and that of an uneducated man on matters requiring delicate discrimination and grasp of thought shows the degree in which the intellect may be fitted by training for tasks of this nature. A large and liberal culture is probably also the best corrective of the tendency to take petty views of things, and on this account is especially to be desired for women on whom it devolves to give the tone to society." *

Equally and even more important a thorough intellectual education seems desirable for the ladies of the upper classes of a people when the fact is considered that upon them devolve the social institutions concerning the weal of the poorer classes, hospitals, hygienic reforms, educational provisions. Here also a clear mind, well trained in thinking, is as essential as a warm heart. That finally an extended course of study, above all things, is necessary for those who are to undertake the office of teaching others, is so obvious that it needs no particular emphasis.

"The incompleteness of the education of schoolmistresses and governesses is a drawback which no amount of intelligence and good-will can enable them entirely to overcome. It is obvious that for those who have to impart knowledge the primary requisite is to possess it; and it is one of the great difficulties of female teachers that they are called upon to instruct others while very inadequately instructed themselves. The more earnest and conscientious devote their leisure hours to continued study, and, no doubt, much may be done in this way; but

---

* E. Davies, The Higher Education of Women, London, 1866, pp. 73, etc.

it is at the cost of overwork, often involving the sacrifice of health, to say nothing of the disadvantages of working alone, without a teacher (often without good books) and without the wholesome stimulus of companionship." *

Miss Davies then refers to the numerous objections in which the men are so inventive when improvement of female education is concerned. She combats them effectually, and then, with clear insight into the want of satisfaction arising from study without guidance and ultimate aim, demands degree-examinations for women in the universities. She expects an improvement in the entire field of female education from such examinations; colleges and preparatory schools would be, she thinks, obliged to take them into account, and, above all, the appointment of teachers would be subjected to a more rigid control, and better teachers would be wanted. She concludes with pointing out that many of those differences between "male and female occupations," "male and female peculiarities," are raised arbitrarily, and derived from the *present* state of affairs; just as she pointed out in the earlier course of her *exposé* that much of what the women demand now used to be granted to them unhesitatingly, so that,

---

* E. Davies, The Higher Education of Women, p. 73.

in fact, the present movement simply intends to recover the former state of affairs, hence that the defenders of the present state are to be considered the reformers. "To create facts," says she, "and then to argue from them as though they were the result of an unalterable destiny is a method which convinces only so long as it is enforced by prejudice. 'Every one according to his capacity!' 'To every laborer that work for which he is best suited!' These are maxims of unquestioned validity. But who shall say for another—much more, who shall say for half the human race—this, or that, is the measure of your capacity; this, and no other, is the work you are qualified to perform? 'Women's work,' it is said, 'is helping work.' Certainly it is! And is it men's work to hinder? The vague information that women are to be ministering angels is no answer to the practical questions, Whom are they to help? And how? The easy solution, that it is their nature to do what men can not do or can not do so well, has never been adopted in practice, inasmuch as everything in the world that there is to do, the care of infants alone excepted, men are doing; and there is nothing that a trained man can not do better than an untrained woman." *

---

* E. Davies, The Higher Education of Women, p. 171.

Miss Davies finally touches the question: What will happen when the women seize upon the occupations of men, and thus injure them? This is a question which appears less urgent than the opposite party would have us believe, since as long as the world will exist the great majority of women will find ample occupation in the care of their families and the education of their children. Their professional engagement will be at best a temporary one, but as such it may prove of the highest usefulness.

"Will not the intrusion of women into professions and trades already overcrowded lower the current rate of wages, and by thus making men less able to support their families, in the long run do more harm than good? As to the manner and degree in which the labor market might be affected by such a readjustment as is proposed it is difficult to predict anything with certainty. It is impossible to tell beforehand how many women would take to what is called (by a very conspicuous *petitio principii*) men's work, and how large a portion of their lives they would devote to it. If women already destined to work for their bread chose to earn it in some hitherto unaccustomed way, it is obvious that in the exact measure in which their entrance into a new profession reduced the rate of wages in that particular calling it would tend to raise it in some other which they would have otherwise pursued, and the balance would thus be restored. If, on the other hand, women are not supporting themselves they are being supported by somebody else, consuming either present earnings or accumulated savings. To keep them from earning money does not prevent their spending it. Let us suppose the event, not a very probable one, that the introduction of women into the medical profession would lower the average rate of remuneration by one third, in which case the professional income of an ordinary medical man would be lessened in the same proportion. Let us suppose also—a not at all improbable case—that the doctor's wife, or sister, or daughter, would earn, in the practice of *her* profession, a sum equivalent to the one third he has lost. Evidently, the doctor and his family would be where they were, neither better nor worse off than before. In the mean time, the public would be so much richer by getting its medical attendance one third cheaper. Whatever might be the temporary effect of opening any particular profession to women one thing is certain it can never be for the interest of society, in a purely economical aspect, to keep any class of its members in idleness. A man who should carry one of his arms in a sling in order to secure greater efficiency and importance to the other would be regarded as a lunatic. The one free member might very probably gain a little extra dexterity of an abnormal sort, but that the man would be, on the whole, a loser, is obvious. The case of the body politic is precisely analogous. The economical argument is all in favor of setting everybody to work. Such difficulties as exist are of a moral or aesthetic nature, and require for their disentanglement considerations of a different sort from those which govern the comparatively easy economical question.*

---

* E. Davies, The Higher Education of Women, p. 173.

CHAPTER II.

FIRST FEMALE COLLEGES IN ENGLAND.

Miss Davies's book only expressed in words what moved in the hearts and brains of many people during the decade in which her book appeared (1866), and the questions touched upon here came up continually in the discussions of the press, and found the unreserved approval and support among influential men. It was at last concluded to make a trial of opening the university courses to woman. In 1869 a house was rented in Hitchin, situated not far from Cambridge, and some of the foremost professors of the university, who had expressed the greatest interest in the experiment, were ready to conduct the studies of female students, despite the enormous sacrifices of time and personal comfort it would involve. In October, 1869, six young women congregated at Hitchin to begin the new and bold undertaking. They were acquainted only with the elements of the ancient languages and mathematics, and the modest requirements of the "little-go"* seemed to them enormous.

After a year of hard work, five of them submitted to this "previous" examination. The examiners had expressed their willingness to test their work according to the standards set up by the university. The result was favorable, and the women who had thus won admission to the further studies of the university now took up the mathematical and classical tripos, and graduated with honor after several years of hard toil and labor. Meanwhile in Girton, near Cambridge, a site for a

---

* The English university examinations consist of "previous" (at least in Cambridge), called "little-go" in student's slang, and "final" examinations, which latter again consist of an easier and a more difficult one. The former, the so-called *degree examination*, secures to the student the degree of "bachelor of arts," and is comparatively easy. In Germany the results of English university education are gauged by its requirements, which seems incomprehensible. But of this ordinary degree the Englishman thinks very little. He who can afford it passes the much more difficult examination "with honors" (called "tripos" in Cambridge). The women nowadays invariably undertake to prepare for this examination "with honors," after having passed the ordeal of the "little-go." They do not care for the degree examination. It is not my business, nor do I feel inclined to discuss the methods of university examination, its many annoyances and unprofitable features. They are made by men, not by women, and are not intimately related with the question at issue. But of course the women have to submit to the institutions as they find them, and must not be made responsible for their existence.

new female college was bought and the erection of a new building begun. The means to this enterprise were raised partly by subscription, partly by a mortgage on the property. "During the time of the erection of the college building," so writes a young American lady, a young Girtonian, from whose report these data are taken,* "students and professors frequently came to the college, and many a stone was laid by them with their own hands. In 1872 the new institution was opened under the name of *Girton College*. In October, 1873, the new buildings were occupied, and since that time the interest of the university of Cambridge has been more generous to its foster-child than ever."

The little report referred to appeared in 1876, hence shortly after the establishment of the new college, at a time in which the university proper had not formally sanctioned the institution, in which consequently everything depended upon the good will of the professors. The reporter can not praise enough the sacrifices made by some members of the university, who willingly gave up their leisure hours in the afternoon in order to come to Girton to give their lessons. Girton had at that time no tutors as yet, who could only be women. After a description

---

* An Interior View of Girton College. Cambridge, 1876.

of the life in college, she finds it difficult to give a clear idea of the healthy tone that prevailed there without raising in her American readers the suspicion that the students had belonged to that strong-minded type which is justly so much abhorred. "Perhaps it can not be stated in any better way why this idea is utterly wrong of Girton College students than by emphasizing that they were not even conscious of their exposed position and representative character. They did not consider themselves at all as leaders in a 'cause'; they hardly ever mentioned among themselves their exposed position before the eyes of the public. They were true-hearted English girls and women, who worked for the sake of work, from their own impulses, with joyful hearts, entirely free of that unwholesome aspiration for recognition so frequently found among women who are engaged in intellectual work. Half of the students intend to become teachers—not governesses, but school teachers and principals. . . . The other half of the students at Girton work without a special profession in mind."

Since the appearance of this report more than twelve years have passed, and Girton College has grown rapidly. The modest building intended only to offer room for nineteen students has been extended and enlarged to a very stately edifice, which offers room for a hundred students. Such a success was possible only by the great and active interest shown everywhere. Women of intelligence and influence, like Lady Stanley of Alderley, Lady Goldsmith, Lady Ponsonby, Miss Davies, Miss Shireff, sacrificed their time and means to this enterprise; several legacies covered a great part of the building expenses; and the future of the college seems now completely secured. According to the report of 1887 one hundred and twenty-nine Girtonians have passed their examinations with honors, namely, forty-four in classical philology, thirty-six in mathematics, one in mathematics and history, twenty-two in natural sciences, two in natural sciences and philosophy, fourteen in philosophy, eight in history, one in modern languages and in theology; besides these, twenty-nine students have passed the degree examination of the common "bachelor of arts" standard.

A remarkably active life—internally and externally—fills the vast building. Those who predicted a complete ruin of health as a consequence of the increased intellectual efforts would be astonished to see, instead of expected pale, hollow-chested, overstudied blue-stockings, fresh young women of blooming color and energetic movements. The extraordinarily liberal supply of food in the college adds undoubtedly to the looks and disposition of the inmates; besides, the work itself is in a high degree animating, inasmuch as it is more the intellect than the memory which is appealed to. Lastly, the reviving effect of fresh air, cold water, and much physical exercise, to which the spacious lawns of the campus, a gymnasium, and the lovely meadows and fields around Cambridge invite urgently—I say a faith in the effect of all this is one of the articles of the Girtonian creed. In all kinds of weather excursions in vehicles, on horseback, or on foot are made daily, and on bright afternoons the balls at lawn-tennis are seen flying to and fro amid the cheerful laughter of the students.

The external discipline is limited to a few rules, absolutely necessary in such a large community; they have reference to coming and going, visits and calls, and similar points. In all else the Girtonians are perfectly free, and the use they make of their liberty shows that they are worthy of it. A certain programme has developed, as it were, of itself. The day begins at seven o'clock; at eight divine service is held in the session room; between 8.15 and nine o'clock breakfast is taken; the remainder of the morning is devoted to study. Some of the students attend the lectures at Cambridge with the young men, or they work with the lady tutors who live in

Girton. Some lectures are given in the afternoon by the professors coming over from Cambridge. Each student receives the greatest consideration possible regarding her individual studies. At times a lecture programme is modified or changed so as to accommodate two students, or even one student. The excellent state of physical health of the students may be accounted for partly by the limitation to which the time devoted to instruction is subjected. Instead of five lessons, as is the custom in our German seminaries, these students have rarely more than two lessons, and that is considered enough, in order to afford ample time for preparation and consultation in private study, which is given great weight. Thanks to the generosity of warm-hearted men and women, everything can be procured that may in any way support this study—a laboratory, a spacious library room (which is being filled rapidly), a reading room, and last, but not least, comfortable private rooms invite to hard study. Each student has two rooms, a study and a bed-room, and with the aid of books, pot plants and flowers, pictures, rugs, and tidies, she makes her rooms a little home of her own. Here the mornings are spent in study if there are no lectures on her programme. Luncheon is served between twelve and three, and work is not taken up again before a good deal of physical exercise in the open air is taken and the mind has been furnished with new elasticity. After dinner, which is served at six o'clock, and consists of nutritious meats, vegetables, and puddings, frequently follows music, and even a little dancing. And again intellectual work is taken up, but the appearance of tea, coffee, or cocoa, brought into the rooms upon neat salvers, interrupts work. At times, a tea-party in one of the private rooms is held, which, compared with the male students' evening amusement behind the flowing bowl, is greatly preferable and causes less headache. Some of the students go to bed at half-past ten, others stay up and study by lamplight till midnight. A healthy modesty prevails in all their studies far from exaggeration, yet it may be claimed that more real work is performed here than in male colleges. Young men, having much superfluous time and energy, squander it in pastimes, and hence it may be deemed a good thing that the tender physical constitution of woman will not admit this double exertion.

The institution is now under the efficient management of Miss Welsh, who was among the first who started the bold enterprise at Hitchin. A vice-mistress, Miss Ward, and a few lady tutors living in the college, are her assistants. For these tutorships the best selections are made. Thus, philosophy is represented by Miss Constance Jones, who passed the examination in that branch with the highest honors, and who, by introducing Lotze into England and by translating his Microcosmos in a masterly manner, has made herself meritorious. For the classics (ancient languages and history) Miss Ramsay has been acquired. She it was who in 1887 won the highest honors in the classical tripos, that is to say, beat her male competitors. She has been introduced to the German female world by an essay of Marie von Bunsen.*

The Times of June 20, 1887, wrote editorially about her: "Indeed, an astonishing performance! Miss Ramsay competed with young men who were known to be the best trained students philologically of the best schools of the country—and she beat them in their own particular domain. Yes, she proved herself superior to them by a whole class; she is not only the first of a class to which several are admitted—no, she is entirely alone in the highest class. To such a distinction no male student ever rose; in no previous year was the difference on the field of classics between the first and second victor so marked as this year. Miss Ramsay has accomplished what no 'senior classic' ever accom-

---

* Die Frau im gemeinnuetzigen Leben, 1888, 1. Heft, p. 69.

plished before." Miss Ramsay was then twenty years old, that is, several years younger than her competitors, but had to comply with all the requirements of examination demanded of the young men. In August, 1889, she married a master of Trinity College, and hence is going to be lost to Girton. It is an interesting fact that the students of Girton and Newnham, after completing their studies, marry soon, and marry men of distinction. Across the channel the idea does not seem to prevail that woman is to begin to learn after marriage "whatever and as much as the beloved husband wants her to know" (Paul de Lagarde). On the contrary, the idea is not so wrong that husband and children will fare better in their inner and outer life if the wife is a thoroughly educated woman.

Shortly after the first trial had been made at Hitchin, and even before Girton College was finished, the establishment of a new college for women was commenced. It was to be erected in Cambridge, and to-day it competes, under the name of *Newnham College*, in a pleasant manner with Girton. Already it offers a comfortable home to over one hundred students. It owes its existence and rapid growth above all to the unselfish endeavors of one of the most distinguished professors of Cambridge, Professor Henry Sidgwick, whose wife is a niece of the Marquis of Salisbury (the present prime minister of England), and also to the present manager of the college, Miss Anne Clough. "This name," so writes a Newnham student, "as the name of one who still lives among us, need not be praised; it must be synonymous with a courage and determination and a love and unselfishness to which in years to come the words of Homer will be applied: 'οὐ γάρ πω τοίους ἴδον ἀνέρας οὐδὲ ἴδωμαι.'" *

This college also found the most abundant support, morally and materially, and hence flourishes. It had to change its domicile several times before it could erect its own buildings. It now consists of three halls; the first was opened in 1875, the second in 1885. The ever increasing number of students led to the erection of a third, which was opened in June, 1889, at which occasion the Prince and Princess of Wales were present. The three buildings are called "The Old Hall," "Sidgwick Hall" (under the management of Miss Gladstone, daughter of the ex-prime minister), and "Clough Hall."

Life passes here in much the same way as at Girton, and under the motherly care of Miss Clough the students live happily and judiciously in performing effective work. The report of 1887 makes

---

* "Such men I never yet saw, and hardly ever shall see." Iliad, I, 262.

known, that, since 1871, one hundred and thirty-nine students have passed their examination with honors, namely, twenty-five in classical philology, twenty-nine in mathematics, thirty-three in natural sciences, eighteen in philosophy, twenty-nine in history, five in modern languages. Besides this a considerable number of women have studied at Newnham different branches according to their own individual needs and inclinations. This is a privilege offered by Newnham which distinguishes it from Girton.

The colleges in Cambridge, however, had still many trials and tribulations to pass through before they could enjoy the general recognition and the secure position which they now enjoy. For ten years the students of the two colleges had been examined unofficially, depending upon the voluntary service of the professors, not upon an admitted right. With the growth of both institutions, both internally and externally, the unsatisfactory state of dependence was keenly felt, and it was urgently desired to acquire a formal right of admission to the university examinations. In Cambridge itself little opposition was to be feared; the blameless deportment and the notable intellectual performances of the lady students had disarmed the greater number of the opponents, and it was certain that among the members of the university living in Cambridge there would be a majority in favor of the proposition. But one of the regulations of an English university is that its graduates are granted a vote in its affairs; and the men, mostly unenlightened country members, were the ones whose prejudices and opposition were feared.

In 1881 a motion was made to formally grant to women the admission to the tripos examinations. This motion was to come to a vote in the senate of the university on the 24th of February. It was seconded by several of the foremost professors. "The 24th," says a small report of Newnham College Commemoration Day, "came at last, and never before were seen so many old-fashioned gowns, that seemed to have lain away unused for years, and whose wearers had hastened from all parts of England to take part in the memorable senate-session. An unusual number of voters were present. Outside, mounted messengers of Girton and Newnham waited in breathless expectation to take the first news to their colleges. To the friends of our cause in the senate the question seemed dubious until the vote was taken and the solemn and ceremonious 'placet' or 'non placet' was pronounced by each voter.

"Even to the most sanguine the result was a

great and joyful surprise, for our cause had won with three hundred and ninety-eight against thirty-two votes; and thus the day was ours. Little was done at Newnham that day, and the groups of expectant students in the halls received the bringer of glad tidings with an enthusiasm that will never be forgotten by those present.

"Though it is true that we are not in possession of all the privileges belonging to university members, for we only condescend to listen to the lectures of the professors, just as they formally condescended to examine us; yet our success so far gives us hope for the future, and now let Newnham's red bricks become stone-gray with age in the proud consciousness that it is no longer an accidence, a stranger, a foundling, but an integral part of the University of Cambridge. That is the great event which has made the 24th of February, 1881, a red-letter day in our calendar."

Perhaps no fact is better suited to illustrate a point than that the English women are never tired of emphasizing, with deep-felt gratitude, the unanimous, unselfish support they found among unprejudiced men.

One more point will have to be mentioned. The university grants *much*, but it does not grant *all*. It recognizes the applicants for licenses, but does not recognize them as full-fledged members of the university—that is to say, it does not grant degrees, such as "bachelor of arts," nor the use of the library, laboratories, and museums, although, in this respect, the kindness of many of the professors have made concessions which are ample enough for practical purposes. That the university denies the *degrees*, that is, the name, while it grants the *thing*, has its cause in the circumstance that with the degree is connected the right to participate in the management of the university, and, in certain cases, even pecuniary advantages. If the degrees were given to women these advantages would have to be shared with them; but, considering the great favor the studying women have found in England, it is not expecting too much when this last concession is hoped to be made ere long.* Especially is this only a question of time, since the University of London has meanwhile offered a good example in this regard and annuled all differences in the rights of male and female students. Since the character of the University of London, which is really only a

---

* How decidedly this is acknowledged on the part of the students is seen from the fact that in the Greek drama, the performance of which is considered an event in Cambridge, a Girtonian had to take one of the female *rôles* in 1885, and Miss Case, of Girton, played the Athene in the Eumenides of Æschylus in December of the same year.

board of examiners, is quite different from that of the ancient universities, the consequences of granting degrees are different also.

The next consequence of the opening of female colleges in Cambridge was the opening of two similar institutions in Oxford, Lady Margaret Hall and Sommerville Hall. Both have essentially the same character as those of Cambridge.

Then followed, in 1878, the very important step mentioned before—the London University opened all its grades to women. Several colleges have since been established in London intended to prepare young women for the university examinations. The lectures in University College are attended by men and women simultaneously, except the purely medical course. Libraries and laboratories are both used in common by both sexes, without any of those inconveniences that were formerly apprehended, since both sexes meet with all the tokens of good society—in fact, the position which the male students have taken in this question is one which betrays a high degree of culture and good breeding. The female students in the University College of London have their own lady superintendent, Miss Morrison, to whom they may appeal for information in all cases; there is no pressure or undue influence exercised upon them in any way.

In order to afford these students the same advantages and conveniences for quiet, undisturbed study that the students at Cambridge and Oxford have, a students' home, College Hall, has been erected in the vicinity of University College. This is under the management of Miss Grove. In this home a number of the female medical school students (of which more anon) have found comfortable quarters. Smaller colleges (like the Westfield College, at Hampstead) try to meet the pressing need felt everywhere in London.

Among the other English female colleges (there are some in Manchester, Cardiff, Bangor, etc.) one deserves special mention, chiefly on account of the incredibly large dimensions of its buildings. It is too young to speak of its results as yet. It is Royal Holloway College, and was opened in presence of the Queen of England in 1886. It can be reached from London in an hour and a half, and is situated in Egham on a little hill in one of the most lovely of English landscapes. The edifices are truly princely. The sum expended in their erection amounts to $3,000,000. They are built in French Renaissance style, and surround two large courts. The length and breadth, respectively, of the enormous rectangular building is 550 and 376 feet. One can form an adequate idea of the colossal size of the building when it is stated that it has about a thousand rooms and three thousand windows. It is designed to accommodate, pleasantly, two hundred and fifty students and teachers with their servants; possesses a chapel of its own; a picture gallery worth $450,000; extensive outhouses used as kitchens, machine rooms for steam-heating, electric light, etc. This college is under the management of Miss Bishop.

The founder of this college, Thomas Holloway, carried out the wishes of his wife, as he expressly states in the document of foundation. The college is, as stated before, too young as yet to point to any results accomplished by it; it has just completed its first year of study, and is obliged to contend with many difficulties yet. But in its grandeur (the founder has since endowed it with funds) it is another eloquent proof of the great and large-hearted interest which the woman's movement has awakened in England.

CHAPTER III.

WOMEN AND THE STUDY OF MEDICINE.

In one faculty only the fight against prejudice and professional jealousy has been violent also in England, namely, in that of medicine. How the woman question plays a *rôle* in the battle for subsistence was shown in the vote upon the admission of women to the degrees of the London University. The greatest liberality was shown by the voters of arts and science faculties (which, in England, are less of bread and butter studies than in Germany), but the most obstinate opposition was raised by the medical faculty. In "arts" the vote was eighty for and twenty against admission of the women; in "science" it was eighty-nine for and eleven against; but in "medicine" it was only twenty-one for and seventy-nine against.

The beginning of studying medicine was made, as is well known, by an English lady in America. Miss Elizabeth Blackwell, in 1844, addressed letters to all the thirteen medical faculties then existing in the United States, praying for admission to the study of medicine. Twelve refused the petition. One, the Geneva Medical College in New York, took the case into consideration and resolved to submit the question to the decision of the students. A meeting was held, and the students decided in favor of admitting her; the students also pledged themselves to treat her as gentlemen would do, so that she might never repent her entering the college. That resolution was carried out. And thus the study of medicine was opened to women in America, though much contention had to be gone through with before the movement gained ground. For there were in the medical faculties in America men enough who spoke of "the unheard-of presumption which had filled the petitioner with the desire and hope to enter a profession which is reserved for the nobler sex;" and others who asserted, "that it was improper and immoral to initiate a woman into the nature and laws of her own organism."

In England, the fight began in 1860. Miss Elizabeth Garrett (now Mrs. Anderson) elected the study of medicine, and since it was generally thought that the case was an isolated one, which would hardly find much imitation or have weighty consequences, she was permitted to pass the required examinations. Although many obstacles were placed in her way, she succeeded, after five years of hard study, to be admitted as a full-fledged physician. When a few other women followed her example, opposition was aroused, and led (especially in Edinburgh, where Miss Jex Blake, in 1869, had been admitted the first female medical student) to very shocking scenes, so that Miss Blake, and other young ladies who had entered after her, went to London, where, with the aid of Mrs. Anderson and Miss Thorne, they tried to establish a college of their own. One of the most zealous supporters of their cause was a young physician, Dr. Anstie, one of the rare, generous men who like to use their enthusiasm and energy in behalf of the oppressed, and to render service to an idea. "In his blood," so writes Robert Wilson in an article on Æsculapia Victrix (from which these data are culled), "was a remarkable dash of the chivalry of the good olden time, which made him known as the Bayard of his profession, the irreconcilable enemy of all in office who use their power and prerogatives in oppressing others. His social qualities, his scientific and literary talents, and the high standing he occupied in the profession, had given a weight to his influence which is rarely conceded to a man of his age, so that when he undertook a "case"—and he was rarely without one—there were always numerous colleagues of his who were ready to help him; and even those who opposed his ideas as Utopian, reduced their opposition as much as possible. From the day on which Dr. Anstie became convinced that Miss Jex Blake and her companions were the victims of mean persecution their battle was half won in London. This is plainly visible in the names of the noted men of science who, on August 22, 1874, came together in his house on Wimpole Street, where it was resolved to establish an independent medical college for women in London, and to place Dr. Anstie at the head of it."

Twenty-four of the foremost physicians formed the board of directors of the new college which was opened in Henrietta (now Haendel) Street in the year 1874. Dr. Anstie, alas, did not live to see that day. He died shortly before—a victim of his profession—of blood-poisoning, contracted in the dissecting-room. The new school was under the management of Dr. Norton till 1883; since then Mrs. Garrett-Anderson, M. D., is the dean.

Naturally the young institution was subject to many annoying circumstances, and even attacks; but it always found, even in the medical profession, generous and unprejudiced men, who supported the brave women in their good cause, who granted them admission to hospitals and good clinics, and thus, within three years, all difficulties were removed. The last and most significant step was the admission of women to all degree examinations and lectures of the London University, since there all sciences related to medicine can be studied freely, and the professional part, the science of medicine proper, is given due attention in a separate college. The financial difficulties also were removed, partly through subscription, partly through the magnanimity and generosity of friends of the cause.

He who visits the school of medicine in Haendel Street to-day will see in the zealously active (and in their activity happy) students, that the hard times are passed; and he who attends a commencement or calls on any other festive occasion will notice the friendly intercourse between teachers and students and the obvious interest men of high position in their profession show in the flourishing institution. The house on such occasions is in festive garment, the dissecting room is securely closed, the different necessary but unæsthetic models and preparations in spirits in the museum are hidden from the gaze of the public; on the lawns, which here as well as elsewhere are inclosed within the college walls, cheerfulness reigns supreme. The foolish prejudice which at first barred women the way to the study of medicine even in England is disappearing more and more, though some physicians of high repute are supporting the prejudice with all the energy at their command.

Robert Wilson, in the book afore-mentioned, says: " Whether most of those who entertained that prejudice are dead, or whether they have become wiser, is difficult to say. English women now study medicine and surgery in London, without the least opposition in their own college, with professors of great repute. . . . And as to 'the world,' which once asserted that such extension of the 'sphere of woman' would ruin society, that same 'world' looks on calmly, apprehending ruin as little as an imitation earthquake in a sensational drama on the stage makes the real world tremble."

But not only "society" but also "womanliness," a word that plays such an important *rôle* among the sham arguments of the opponents, is in no danger from the study of medicine, as experience clearly proves. More than that, the "womanliness" of a great number of patients is spared. In nothing is seen clearer what nonsense the thoughtless public trained by long continued experience is able to believe and to defend. Many things, especially in the social intercourse of the sexes, are considered unwomanly which have not the least objectionable feature in them; on the other hand, things have become firmly established customs which are only bearable because we have accustomed ourselves to them. The same young lady who, by the inexorable social laws, claims the most tender consideration in physical as well as other respects, is obliged to submit her physical being to very minute examination by a strange man. The contradiction and absurdity which lies in this will only be understood by future generations, who will have a different conception of " womanliness" than ours. There will be a time in which everything will be considered as belonging to woman's sphere that arises from the depths of love and sympathy, of which, God be thanked, our sex is rich. Yes, love and sympathy are the mainsprings of that passive strength which enables the women of England to patiently wait for a better time to come. " Because we believe that the medical profession offers room and work for woman and affords the most womanly gifts and virtues opportunities for display, a fact which is getting to be generally understood, a new group of women, though small, but filled with the deepest concern, will matriculate as students of medicine. It would probably be a surprise to the public (as it was to the present writer) to see how extraordinarily insignificant is the amount of 'strong-mindedness' (in the common acceptation of the word) among the women who devote their lives to medicine. And the fact that this unlovable quality shines rather by its absence than by its presence, might, if it were generally known and valued, lead thinking people to contemplate how little the apparent cause of the reproach is derived from the position into which the pioneers of the movement have been placed by arbitrary and unchivalrous opposition." *

Never has a truer word been said. We shall have to make the experience, doubtless, in even greater degree here in Germany, where the opposition of men against a higher education of the female sex is more bitter and determined, since the battle for subsistence is fiercer. On that account the women will have to resolve to fight a hard fight, which may not at all be in harmony with their natural inclination, but which becomes a matter of conscience and necessity on behalf of their own sex, and during which many men will have opportunities of pointing to the "unwomanliness of the movement." Alas, many women will be found to join them in this denunciation.

In England, the party of those who consider the medical profession unwomanly is fast disappearing.

---

* Woman and Medicine. A prize essay, by Edith A. Huntley. 1886.

"No educated and unprejudiced man believes to-day that the medical profession or its practice must necessarily demoralize woman. To attend the sick has at all times had a peculiar and, it seems, very natural charm for women; hence it is simply contrary to common sense to suppose that a woman is compromised in this service, and that she should render it only when it can be done without professional preparation, in fine, without science. And yet these queer people 'who would rather see their daughters in their coffins' than in a sick-room, save when it is in the *rôle* of nurses, would make us believe it. . . . They are wedded to the idea that the presence of a woman at a sick-bed must needs injure a woman's character if she is not too ignorant to find out what is the cause of the disease. But they deceive no one. As Emerson says, in his English Traits, most Englishmen are godless in their skepticism against a theory, but they kiss the ground before a fact. Now, what is the fact in this case as most enlightened men see it? Well, for eleven years women have studied and practiced medicine in England, supported by public opinion, without having lost in society one iota of respect as daughters, women, and mothers, or without having shown the least degeneration with regard to the nobler qualities of heart and mind. *Cadit questio.* The majority of Englishmen unquestionably think, with the lamented Grote, that a woman who shows in her youth real love of learning and genuine aspiration, and thus becomes able to support herself, should have at least the same good chance that a man has to make use of her talents as much as possible."*

Now, what has actually been gained in England in medicine? What are the chances for women who select the medical profession? According to the latest report of the London School of Medicine for Women (1888), sixty women have thus far been entered, by state authority, upon the list of approved physicians. Some of them practice medicine under favorable circumstances in England, some in other parts of Europe, and quite a number in India. But as yet there seems to be no occasion to make the profession an object of selfish speculation. And it is well that it is so—that thus far genuine enthusiasm and determined will to bear privation and trouble for a good cause are necessary to women who choose the medical profession. It is interesting to read what Mrs. Garrett-Anderson says on that point. "We know very well that the call for female physicians does not come from the *highest* stratum of society, but from the best educated and the *poorest* people. They are not wanted by the little trades-

---

* Æsculapia Victrix, p. 31.

people nor by indolent fashionable ladies. There are two strata of society which offer physicians a practice: First, the poor, presumably because the eternal melancholy state of their lives undermines their health; the poor are, as is well known, the consumers of medicine 'par excellence'; second, the rich, indolent women, who take little medicine but like consultations with their pleasant-spoken, cheerful physician. These latter can be designated as paying patients; poor women *take* medicine, and rich women *pay for it*. But it is reasonable to suppose that to this class of patients female physicians will never be as acceptable as male physicians. Now if one deducts all the 'fine ladies,' all men, and almost the entire middle class, it becomes obvious that it will take a long time to obtain a practice. Nothing is left but the very poorest people and the professional class, but this latter is in truth the highest aristocracy. But even here are obstacles. People who would not be barred by prejudice to confide to a female physician just entering the profession, usually have a male family physician, whom to dismiss they would justly hesitate, if he has done his duty to them. And then beginners in the profession naturally meet with distrust, or if not that, want of confidence. To this comes a social difficulty—to get acquainted. Every young practitioner feels this,

No person is apt to confide in a perfect stranger; he must be known, or, at least, be heard of. The most superficial acquaintance often suffices to make people consult a medical person, probably because most people believe in their skill in reading characters; and though they have seen the physician only once, they feel to a certain degree whether they can confide in him or not. Owing to all these causes, it is certain to my mind that a woman, though she be ever so well prepared professionally, will need to go through a certain time of probation before she can obtain a practice. But I doubt not that such a woman, after a reasonable lapse of time, will gain her point."

To all these difficulties, enumerated by Mrs. Anderson, may be added this one: The female physicians have had, at least until the present time, little opportunity to obtain that part of their professional training which can begin only after the completion of their studies. "When a young man has graduated and passed all his examinations he tries to gain valuable experience by accepting a position as assistant physician in a hospital before he settles down to practice his profession or accepts a responsible position. But there are only few and insignificant possibilities of that kind for a woman graduate. When she has graduated, and is in possession of her diploma, she is at once a full-fledged physician, and it is possible that she be placed in a responsible position immediately. Of course, here she is placed on the same level with men of experience and professional reputation; every error she commits is regarded and spoken of as what women can do and can't do. However, all that must be expected, though it makes the practice of medicine a very difficult and responsible one for women. Women who undertake the work must feel the deepest concern; must be determined not only to prepare for the examinations, but for the most earnest responsibility, for which there is no superficial preparation, no royal roads, no short cuts. They must expect to be subject, for a long time after graduation, to trials and tribulations, to tests of critical eyes and unkind ears, of microscopes and multiplying glasses applied diligently at every error committed. For a long time to come they will have to fight an unequal fight; but their work is worth wrestling for, and their battle, if battle there must be, worth being fought. Perhaps a future generation will read with astonishment of the old dispute about the question of 'female physicians,' and scarcely believe that there has ever been such a dispute. Meanwhile only honest, patient, plodding work, not controversy, can win the victory."

Despite all the difficulties mentioned and others slighted, a good deal of work has been performed in England. Already, hospitals are in operation exclusively for women, managed only by women. The present author will never forget an old laboring woman in the New Hospital for Women in London (managed by Mrs. Garrett-Anderson), who had been in "many a 'orspital," and who, just being operated upon by lady physicians, could not praise the fact loud enough that at last women were beginning to think of their own sex. She had doubtless been treated conscientiously in other hospitals, and her loudly expressed gratitude could only be explained by the comparatively greater comfort of her environments. Nowhere were flowers and pictures wanting; as far as possible the impression of home was made upon the patient. To the hospital mentioned physicians of the foremost rank make visits, and whenever the lady physicians desire, they are ready to come for consultations.

In many cities dispensaries are under female management, and, according to the judgment of Englishmen, the time is not far distant in which all hospitals, schools, dispensaries, workhouses, asylums, prisons, reform schools, emigration ships, etc., will have their officially appointed female physicians.

When that time comes the chances of the profession will greatly improve.

That it should be overcrowded ere long is not to be anticipated for several reasons. First, the study of medicine is a difficult, expensive study—one which requires much time; hence it will never become fashionable. On the other hand, it must be borne in mind that many of the female physicians marry—Robert Wilson claims that the majority of them do. " Indeed, one would almost think that men, in queer contrariness, marry the type of women whose intellectual inclinations they abhor; perhaps because they cunningly consider marriage the easiest solution of the problem of competition." The greatest number of the married female physicians apply their professional knowledge for the benefit of their families, and thus, within a limited sphere, do much good. The few who keep up their profession after marrying are found to deserve the same respect as housewives and mothers that they deserve as physicians. The energy and sense of duty, so well developed in their studies and profession, seems to double their strength. And, finally, the demand for female physicians will before long increase so rapidly that an overcrowding of the profession will not take place in the near future. England has an extended and desirable field in India;

desirable not in a pecuniary point of view, but in the highest degree desirable for those who think that alleviating misery and decreasing unbearable oppression is the task of woman. Only recently the terrible fate of Hindoo women has become the object of general sympathy, and with great energy English women are working to alleviate it; with their medical aid they hope to combine information and intellectual assistance in every respect. Since to them alone free admittance to the harems and zenanas is granted, their influence is very great. A society under the protectorate of the Queen has been formed, in answer to urgent calls of Lady Dufferin, to secure female physicians for India. Since, at the same time, the instruction of Indian girls, which was formerly given by Brahmans, is more and more intrusted to the hands of women (schools have been established in India which are exclusively under female supervision), it is to be hoped that in the course of time Indian women may be in a different position from the one in which they have been for thousands of years.

Thus, in every direction, to woman is opened a bright look into the future.

Of course, even in England there is an occasional opposition; there are women who predict the ruin of their sex, men who predict the ruin of science, but they become rarer every year. For the position of the educated gentlemen in the woman question a speech of Lord Granville, Chancellor of the London University, is significant. He spoke in June, 1888, before an assembly which deliberated upon ways and means of procuring sufficient means for College Hall, the home of London female students. The Times of June 30 reports him to have said: "Many years after I first entered public life, any one who intended to preface a subject such as we, with permission of the Lord Mayor, shall discuss to-day, would have been obliged to mention many things that are perfectly superfluous to-day. The chairman would then have been obliged to call attention to the fact that although a certain faith exists which denies that woman has a soul, it is generally more probable that she has not only a soul, but also a mind; that if she has a mind, it might presumably be improved by education. He might have dared to make a shadowy allusion to the possibility that education and training might do for the female intellect what it did for the male" (hilarity); "but as a sensible man he would have followed the advice which was given to George Stevenson, not to aim too high, and not to admit that a woman could win academic degrees as well as a man any sooner than he would admit that a locomotive could ever run faster than fifteen miles an hour. But the days follow one another without resembling one another. I am sure there is no one in this building to-day who will deny that the highest education given under rational conditions to woman will be of advantage to herself as well as to the community." ("Hear, hear!") "But I will not anticipate those who will speak to you with conviction of the desirability of higher education for women—*a fact of which we, as I confidently suppose, are all agreed.* I will restrict myself to introducing the discussion of the practical and urgent question, how a comfortable and secure home (the previously mentioned College Hall) may be founded for such women who are desirous of making use of the higher education offered in University College and the Woman's Medical School."

The chairman then remarked that indisposition prevented Sir Henry Acland from being present on this occasion; he was a man who merited the highest praise for his support of the cause of higher education for women. To judge from his written utterances, he would have expressed his conviction "*that sufficient means must be procured in order to give women as good an education as men.*" ("Hear, hear!" and "Bravo!") "I may be permitted," continued Lord Granville, "to congratulate the students of College Hall for their conduct, their intellectual accomplishments, and their results. May their work not only be crowned with all the honors which the university can bestow, but may that work be favored by a long, happy, and useful life!"

Thus speaks the Chancellor of the University of London!

This was about the same time in which members of the Prussian House of Deputies, who were called upon to discuss a bill important for the women of Prussia, remarked, " The world will not go to wreck and ruin if the women have to wait a little longer."

CHAPTER IV.

FEMALE SECONDARY SCHOOLS IN ENGLAND.

WHILE thus occupied with the *highest*, that is, the *professional education of women*, people in England by no means forgot the *secondary schools for girls*. On the contrary, their reform was undertaken with rare energy, and in the course of less than two decades a grand and complete revolution has taken place.

Two circumstances have greatly facilitated the task which English women had set themselves. First, no man thought of disputing their right to the education of girls and the management of their schools. The feeling that for girls' education and instruction women above all should be qualified, and the idea that in many cases they alone are qualified, generally prevails. Women have a seat and vote in the municipal school boards. In London people insisted that they should be appointed because some citizens said: Don't we send girls to school? Hence the difficulty, which with us is greatest, did not present itself at all in England. It must be admitted that the management of such schools by women had frequently been quite insufficient, but the cause of this was clear, the women had not been trained sufficiently. Hence adequate provisions for a thorough professional preparation were made. In Germany the authorities came to a different conclusion. Woman's management of schools, as Dr. Nöldeke quotes disdainfully in his book From Weimar to Berlin, has been proved incompetent; hence man must take her place. It shall not be denied for a moment that man did this in the most conscientious manner, but it should be emphatically stated that that was a mischievous mistake. Other people have said enough on that head.* That, however, the natural inclination comparatively rarely induces the men to devote themselves to girls' education, and that bread and butter has something to do with it may be seen from the fact that in Prussia about 14 per cent of the unendowed private girls' schools are managed by men, 86 per cent by women; while of the well-endowed public girls' schools, on the other hand, 92 per cent are managed by men, and only 8 per cent (mostly Catholic ones) by women.

---

* Die hoehere Maedchenschule und ihre Bestimmung. Berlin, Appelius, 1888.

[A graphic presentation will show this significant fact more clearly.— TRANSLATOR.]

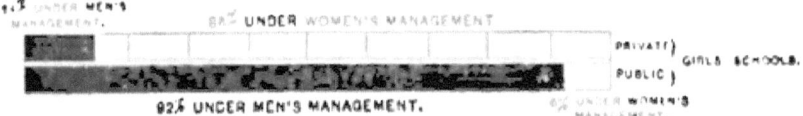

The second circumstance which made the work of reform in England so much more easy is the vital fact that the middle and highest schools (that is, secondary instruction and the universities) in England are free from governmental supervision and interference. That may in certain cases be a great disadvantage, but it may equally often be of advantage. It depends greatly upon the initiative power of the people. We have experienced both in Prussia, the advantage and the disadvantage. There have been times in which the entire school system was elevated by a minister of public instruction who had a proper and correct conception of what the nation needed; we have had times also in which we experienced a reaction that caused deep wounds and badly disfiguring scars.

The development of English life has been such that the cultured strata of society would scarcely tolerate a state guardianship in the education of their children. Noted educational men, among whom Rev. Edward Thring, have made bitter opposition even to the management of the lower schools by the Government. "For the first time in English history," he says disdainfully, "a despotic power lays tracks for the human mind, and demands that they be used by all; and, furthermore, that all, in the name of freedom and enlightenment, be coerced to pay for it."

The discussion of the underlying principle, whether it is more correct and safer to leave the educated classes of society to come to an agreement among themselves as to the scope and measure of their children's education, and only exercise a certain control by means of examinations, occasional refusal, or grant of certain privileges, or whether detailed prescriptions and minute supervision will lead to better results lies outside the scope of this paper. But it is obvious that in the case under discussion, where girls' education is concerned—a thing which is and naturally can be undertaken with enthusiasm only by women—absolute freedom of action was a great advantage to the English women. That, however, a certain uniformity was desirable, such as is procured by governmental supervision, became clear very soon. This was secured by founding a society of great extent. In 1871 (chiefly through the endeavors of Mr. William Gray) a number of men and women came together and founded the National Society for improving the Education of

Women of all Classes. This long title was later on abbreviated to Women's Education Union. Lord Littleton interested himself vigorously in this union, and it is chiefly owing to his efforts that Princess Louise, Marchioness of Lorne (the sister of our Empress Frederick, whose intense interest in all educational matters she shares) consented to occupy the chair. She has since indefatigably worked in behalf of the society, which has some of the best names of England on its roll of membership.

One of the main objects the society had in view was the establishment of good public day schools for girls—that is, day schools in contradistinction to boarding schools. To this end, a company was formed in London, the Girls' Public Day School Company, which opened a number of schools after the model of the excellent private school of Miss Francis Buss. The necessary capital was subscribed rapidly, and now that the company has thirty-two such schools in activity it yields a considerable dividend. Up to March, 1888, these schools in London had 20,837 enrolled pupils, 32 lady principals, 348 class teachers, and 130 special teachers. The salary of the principal or manager consists partly of a fixed annual sum, partly of a percentage of the income, which is determined by the number of pupils, so that it may vary between £300 and £700 ($1,500 and $3,500). Such an income is sufficient for a comfortable living even in England. The sum total paid for salaries was for 1888 £66,618 ($333,090); and for scholarships and prizes the sum of £1,162 ($5,810) was paid. That certainly is a private enterprise which deserves respect.

This example was soon imitated in all parts of England. Other societies were founded which had essentially the same object in view, and the number of *high schools for girls*—that is the commonly accepted name—is estimated to be one hundred and fifty. Their number is steadily increasing. They exercise a healthy influence upon the private schools, and many a poor private school has given way to them.

The high schools had, above all, the intention of removing those faults that the former girls' schools had justly been charged with, and which became so glaring by the examinations mentioned in the foregoing chapters—want of thoroughness and facility in the elements, want of system, negligence and glittering superficiality, waste of time in favor of mere "accomplishments," utter want of organization, etc. It can not be doubted that this has been accomplished; one can not charge the present girls' high schools with the foregoing faults. The managers (principals) have a thorough education; special studies are not insisted upon for these ladies. On the contrary, it is thought preferable that they should have an education which would enable them to estimate the value of special studies rather than overestimate them, and persons are preferred who have had opportunities to learn something more than the routine of the school-room. For the teachers no definitely prescribed preparation is required and no examinations are obligatory as in the state public schools (the so-called "board schools"). There are, however, special normal schools for female teachers of middle and higher schools (in Cheltenham, London, and Cambridge). Many teachers (their number is increasing) receive their professional education here, while others, notably those for the higher grades, go through a university course and take the place of the former male teachers (university graduates). Some of them pass the examination in the theory, history, and practice of education arranged for, since 1880, in Cambridge and in London; but this is not obligatory. The teacher may acquire her knowledge exclusively in a private way; many of them, especially those for modern languages, do it by a sojourn in foreign countries.

The Englishman pays great attention to methods. Especially for the German methods as applied in primary schools and developed in such a high degree, he has great respect. To study these methods male and female teachers come to Germany every year; the best that can be found is collected and made use of after their return. The decided disinclination against the often made proposition to make obligatory a certain technical, that is, professional preparation or the examinations mentioned above, has its cause in the undeniable fact that such an institution is likely to terminate in routine derogatory to the development of an effective individuality. Hence the professional training and the manner of acquiring it is left free. Whether that is best or not may be left undecided here. Suffice it to say that the arguments brought out in the discussion of this question have a certain justification. If comparatively rarely pedagogical mistakes are noticed in these schools, and rarely violations of educational principles (among which violations we may class the lecture mania of the academic teacher in Germany), it would seem as though great care is taken in the selection of teachers and managers. During my visits in these schools I nowhere found a case of lecturing over the heads of the pupils.

In a lecture on English girls' schools recently delivered in Berlin, it was alleged that dictating played an important *rôle* in them, and that the teachers at their desks were surrounded by piles of books—reference and text books. I can not contradict this experience as a personal one; neither can I confirm it, since within the time of my visits (I heard about fifty to sixty lessons in these schools and English colleges) I never had an opportunity for observing it. I did not hear a single sentence dictated. It seems to me that we have here a case of too liberal application of a few individual observations. It would be committing the same error if I should assert nothing was ever dictated in these girls' schools. For in the old English school-system dictation lessons were the backbone of the instruction. I suspect the evil is not entirely unknown even among us, but to-day the school authorities in England condemn it strongly, and, in fact, all mechanical drilling. Take it all in all, the instruction is thorough and is skillfully given; especially in the upper grades I found a very original and spirited manner of treating the subject in hand, a method which would take up a difficulty in an unusual manner and thus awaken interest.

Among the professional women in England—teachers, managers, physicians—whom I have had occasion to observe in large meetings that needed skillful management, parliamentary and otherwise, one will invariably notice now a greater independence and originality than was wont to be found twenty years ago in the typical English lady. Her more thorough education, her energetic work—in which she is supported by good and wise men—has matured a self-consciousness and a large-hearted view of the world which contrasts favorably with the abhorred "emancipation" in manners of former times. It is simply the proof of our thesis. "Man grows with his ever higher aims." To us this opens a delightful view. Our time will come— and we need not fear competition as soon as the one thing is granted to us that is needed—to call into activity the latent powers, liberty for labor and a suitable field for it.

Though the circumstances mentioned prove their reformatory power first upon women who stand within the professions, it is unquestionable that a much more penetrating reform will result from them upon social life, especially since many women of the highest classes evince the intensest interest in the movement. If social and caste prejudices, religious intolerance, and, above all, deeply rooted traditions have hitherto played so important a *rôle* in England (otherwise politically so free), the women may be said to be the cause —that is, the narrow-minded women who grew up in prejudices of all kinds But it is the women also who have caused or begun the happy reform.

But let us go back to our subject, the high schools. Let me try to sketch their organization and the system of instruction found in them, and give utterance to my opinion concerning them.

A German visitor is struck by two things at once. First, of course, as I said before, the management lies entirely in the hands of women; second, the selection of studies.

At the head of every English high school stands a female principal. The teachers of the school are women also, though for some branches men are engaged who stand in no very close connection with the school. Male teachers are not prohibited on principle, but men are never engaged if suitable women can be had. This holds good only for these girls' high schools; in colleges attended by adult women the branches are about equally divided among male and female professors. In the universities the principal studies are all represented by men, since the lectures are designed for and attended by both sexes—a system which is to be approved.

Well, how does the system do that is followed in the middle schools? *Can* women really alone, without male assistance, manage large public schools? The actual results leave it without a shadow of doubt. The administrative business, for which in Germany even well-meaning representatives of the interests of women propose a technical manager, is conducted admirably. The discipline is excellent and is maintained with few and simple means. A notable air of good-breeding prevails amid all harmless gayety, and a complete absence of that defiant tone noticed among girls in schools managed by men. The clock-work of a large school organism moves with noiseless steadiness; the intercourse between teachers and pupils is in by far the greatest number of cases friendly and hearty; the moral conduct is excellent. Strict honesty toward the teachers is a requisite of the good tone of these schools; this honesty is deserved by the confidence offered to the children as long as they do not show themselves unworthy of it.

If the picture I have been delineating differs advantageously from that which German colleagues often present of female teachers in their schools, there is a good cause for it. The English teacher and principal enjoys unquestioned authority, externally and internally. In German public girls' schools the older students know, or instinctively feel, that the education of the female teacher, obtained in a normal school, is despised by the male teachers who obtained theirs in the university. It is too obvious that the women are found only in subordinate positions (exceptions not counted) of the school organism.* No wonder that the pupils sometimes refuse them the respect which is offered as a matter of course in England, where the female teachers are provided with the highest professional education. A harsher tone on the part of the teacher than would otherwise be necessary is the inevitable result. When women can teach, as in England, and God be thanked in German private schools also, as long as life is granted them, the remark of Hermann Oeser holds good: "I take it for granted that many a female teacher, who asserts her authority by a sharp tongue, if her male colleagues do not trust in her disciplinary power, would under changed and better circumstances not take love for weakness, nor rigidity in discipline for strength." Let us create such circumstances; let us give our teachers a sufficient education, and outwardly that

---

* In No. 7 of Buchner's Journal for Female Education (1888) a manager of a girls' school remarks incidentally: It is well known that female teachers in higher public schools for girls have no leading influence. The remark is in harmony with the actual facts, alas! To a foreigner this must appear like irony. Female teachers to have no decisive influence in girls' schools! This Journal for Female Education, compared with the more liberal conduct of the other journal entitled Girls' Schools (Hessel and Doerr), has generally taken a position in regard to female teachers which can not be harmonized with its title. But its manner in arguing can only be useful to our cause.

influential position to which they are entitled, and the lamentation of vindictiveness, acidity, want of discipline, or whatever is charged against them by their colleagues, will soon be silenced.

Hence, that girls should be managed by women, that women should play the *leading rôles* in girls' education, can only be approved; the question is, Is the exclusive appointment of female teachers desirable? I have repeatedly asserted that I am not of that opinion. I value the acuteness of intellect in man too highly to deprive our girls of it; I acknowledge that the instruction given by man is, owing to his peculiar and to the girl unfamiliar mode of thinking, beneficial and stimulating; provided, always, he moves in domains in which the individuality of woman does not appear necessary; that is to say, provided that the man does not teach branches for which, with untrained girls, similarity of thought and feeling and perfect comprehension of the girls' nature are indispensable conditions of success. Hence I should desire a co-operation of men and women in the instruction of girls, of course in such a manner that women should have the authoritative positions, as would seem but natural. This condition of affairs actually exists in German private schools for girls, and the satisfaction it finds justifies it.

Compare the two systems, and we shall come to the conclusion that the English public girls' high schools are preferable to the German. Better far, it would seem, to place the growing generation of girls in the hands of women entirely—a partiality which finds an analogy in boys' schools exclusively managed by men—than the unnatural state of affairs which puts men into leading positions and the women into subordinate ones, and leaves the latter without scientific professional training. We have thus far in Germany bred among female pupils an over-valuation of men and an under-valuation of women teachers and of female capacities. This is injurious to the girls' development of individuality, portentous also to the fulfillment of their future duties. The development of the noblest female qualities, which is always dependent upon good example, is thus not only not facilitated but even hindered. Therein lies the great wrong done our higher public girls' schools.

Considered as an experiment, the English system is also very interesting. That which in Germany is denied not only by men but also by women (this proves how little they study the schools of foreign countries), namely, the *possibility*, is in England actually in existence. Women there manage without the least male assistance large girls' schools which are in no way behind our public schools, yes, even give a scientific education more extended than ours. Women there prove fully competent for the tasks arising from organization, instruction, administration and discipline. They do not shrink from addressing large assemblies of pupils, for which German pedagogues consider the women incapable. All that can be observed in Germany also, since large private schools are here managed by women; but they are always mentioned as "exceptions," and it is taken for granted that a man must necessarily be their regent. Such fictions can not be upheld in the light of facts as reported.

The management by women makes itself felt to the German visitor of an English high school in some characteristic peculiarities. It is to be traced back to female influence that a society has been formed for the purpose of decorating school-rooms. It is the intention of depriving them of the barrack-like appearance. The pupils themselves start window-gardens (with pot-plants), or they collect minerals and shells or adorn their class-rooms with pictures. Even the fireplace is filled in summer with groups of ferns or large leafy plants. Is it not as though we heard Montaigne say, "The school-room floor should be strewn with flowers"?

Attention is paid to everything pertaining to

health. The school-room furniture is made according to the best system. Each pupil has her own desk and seat built according to hygienic rules. Excellent devices for ventilation furnish fresh air, which is "consumed" in England in incredible quantities. The present writer admits that her German constitution proved unequal to the cross-fire of two or three powerful draughts that played upon her during her presence.

As in colleges, so in high schools much is done for bodily exercise; this is partly done by gymnastics in which all the girls are exercised daily, though it may not be longer than half an hour. Especial care is devoted to cleanliness. The arrangements in wash and dressing rooms are exemplary. One extraordinarily practical provision seems to be, that every child is obliged to take off her boots and put on a pair of low shoes without heels when she comes to school. These slippers are placed in a long row of numbered pigeon-holes when the children go home. Of course the better filled English pocket-book explains many things which "we can not understand."

Some few things in these high schools, which may not be peculiarly English, yet are in vogue all over England, did not find my approval; thus, for instance, frequent examinations, public rewards and prizes, "golden rolls" (merit lists) and similar things, all seemed to me hazardous. Some principals have greatly reduced them in number, and, since these things are not the result of uniform rules, it is possible to reform readily. But public opinion clings to examinations and the marking system so pertinaciously that it will not do to remove them; examinations at least will be left to determine promotions, and hence influence instruction.

The courses of study of English high schools require, like the German gymnasium, an attendance till the eighteenth or nineteenth year of age, and since the English girl does not enter the social world before that age, she is frequently kept in school, though she may be excused from a few branches.

As to the instruction itself, it must be stated that the very first elementary work, reading, writing and number work, is not done in these schools, but in Kindergartens (sic! Translator), which are but rarely in organic connection with the preparatory departments of high schools. The pupils enter the latter when eight years old. During the first few years of the high school course, about the same branches are taught as with us, only that English does not play the same *rôle* that with us German plays. The number of hours per week is smaller, since Saturday is a holiday. When about twelve years old the pupils take up Latin and mathematics, to which branches an ever increasing amount of time and energy is devoted, although not quite as much as is required in boys' schools. The time is gained at the expense of the instruction in the mother tongue and foreign modern languages, frequently also at the expense of history. A normal course of study has not been prescribed for all the girls' high schools, since it was deemed wiser to leave free elbow-room to the individuality of the managers. That despite this there is an approximation of uniformity is owing to the fact that the pupils frequently submit to the "junior and senior" examinations, and the fact that many of these students, after graduating from the high school, enter the university, explains the preponderance of classical and mathematical studies in the upper grades.

The same Latin and Greek authors are read (Greek is an optional study) as with us. In geometry Euclid is finished to Book XI; in algebra they go to quadratic equations. In the upper grades many studies are optional.

"One has every reason," says Dr. C. Schoell in Schmidt's Encyclopaedie (2d edition, vol. 3, p. 1130), "to be satisfied with the results of these schools. They insist upon thoroughness in instruction and shunning mere empty show. The results of examination in the different branches, such as Bible knowledge, geography, mathematics, German, have been, so far, very satisfactory. . . . Experience has proved that good women do not fall behind men in circumspect management, in discipline, and in imparting knowledge." This expression, being that of a man, has double value inasmuch as Schoell's criticism of English schools is generally very sharp.

But there is one reflection in regard to these high schools which I can not dismiss. They have a right, certainly, to expect to be judged by their results, and these consist unquestionably in a thorough intellectual education. No doubt that much can be done and that much is done. It is precisely what has been aimed at and what has been accomplished in boys' schools. But is that system justified? Should a formal intellectual education be end and aim of any school? I must go farther back to answer that question.

CHAPTER V.

MORAL EDUCATION IN ENGLAND AND GERMANY.

THERE is a charming French fairy-tale told by Jean Macé. It tells of a little boy who was always the first in school and had learned wonderful things there: he knew when Rome was founded, could distinguish a principal sentence from a relative clause, and knew the governmental departments of the Loire by memory as though he had them on a string. He had a little girl friend who had learned but one thing: "*Il faut obéir au bon Dieu et être bon comme lui avec tout le monde*" (One must obey the good God and be good like Himself to every one). The boy, of course, soon finds that his little friend is hardly a suitable playmate for him. A kind fairy takes both by the hand and leads them first to a great historian, then to the foremost authoress of the land; finally she transports them through time and space into future ages, and into the center of Africa, which then is the most civilized country on the face of the earth.

Everywhere the boy is abashed. The historian shows him how little his knowledge about the foundation of Rome is confirmed; the authoress laughs at his statements of grammar-rules, and nobody knows anything of the departments of the Loire in those future ages, simply because they have disappeared during a great earthquake in the year 2500 after Christ. But every one bows down before what the little girl has learned, and even after thousands of years the highest wisdom is: "*Il faut obéir au bon Dieu et être bon comme lui avec tout le monde.*"

That is, reduced to a formula: Moral truth is more important than knowledge.

But that does not end the matter. The question now arises: What is moral? *How far* and *how* can it influence the will of the child? And, lastly, what has school to do with it? What is moral? The child in the fairy-tale says: "*Il faut obéir au bon Dieu et être bon comme lui avec tout le monde.*" The philosopher says: Moral is that which has become the practice of the majority, and by means of which the greatest possible happiness is secured to mankind.

The two sentences are related to each other like the ideal and the attainable. To be good like God to every one is acting to man like Providence. It presupposes divine perfection, omniscience, and infinite wisdom. That is unattainable, though it should direct our aspirations. And it is well that humanity should forever have an unattainable aim an ideal. The way to it is shown by those who have a heart full of divine pitying love. They are the greatest of mankind. To them we look up; we honor them like gods; "their example teaches us to believe in God."

To do what has become the practice of the majority and will secure the greatest possible happiness to all—that is attainable, at least in thought The principles according to which we must fashion our actions to gain that end, men seek by hard intellectual work; in their coarsest form the statute law expresses them. The errors and faults of the law make appear the idea or conception of morality for the time being, which idea always depends upon the intellectual standpoint reached. This leads us on to morality, religion, science.

The close relation between morality and intellect is a truth which the fairy-story can not teach us; in this, as in so many other things, a sharp definition must be made possible by analysis, before a conclusion by synthesis is reached. For us adults, however, the statement that for true morality not only will-power but also judgment is necessary, and a correct estimation of things, persons, actions, and ideas, seems a hackneyed truism. An *auto da fé* does not appear moral to us, though it be dictated by the purest of convictions; even the senseless self-sacrifice of a mother who by her action brings up an egotistical weakling of a son, can not appear moral to us, however much we may value self-sacrifice.

Mankind in its infancy could believe the moral and intellectual parts of its spiritual life as independent of each other, we know to-day they can hasten progress only if combined : " *That* we want to do our duty is the moral part ; that we know *how* to do it is the intellectual part. The closer the two are connected with each other, the greater will be the harmony with which they act, and the more minutely the means correspond with the object in view, the more completely our life's destiny will be reached, and the more securely the conditions for further progress of mankind are secured." Thus speaks Buckle in his principal chapters on this point.

Though logical thinking and a wide intellectual horizon are essential factors of genuine moral action, they by no means alone lead us to morality. If they did, intellectual culture would not, since Rousseau, have been so often coupled with the direst immorality. There must be added to intellectual culture a habit of applying it in the dominion of morality—that is, the intellectual factor must be brought to the other chief factor: moral will-power. And that leads us to the second question: How far and in what way can the will-power be influenced in the child?

The answer lies in the foregoing. Such an influence can be exercised directly through religious instruction, but it can, indirectly, take place also in a roundabout way through the intellect; the proper comprehension must be awakened. In neither case must instruction be abstract. The child dislikes preaching. But it is open always to the effect of imagination and enthusiasm. Hence the great effect of examples, symbols, and poetry. Moral will-power is best kindled by examples of high noble men in history, both Biblical and profane, and in poetry.

Our third question is: What has school to do with it? Many think it has nothing to do with it. With them school is a knowledge-factory, and is to offer even that which prepares for the children's future callings; hence, with them school is designed to be professional. According to the greatest educators, however, it has an entirely different duty to perform, and that duty becomes all the more imperative since family influence is weakening in an alarming degree. School can systematically influence the development of will-power and aid the liberation of the thinking power; it is done best by inducing the pupils to observe human life and action. Human life is to be the object of our knowledge, the intellect is to be trained, true judgment to be gained by studying life; in the course of human life the effect of moral laws is shown.

Some time ago, I advocated the teaching of a special branch of study, "Knowledge of life"; if not the name, the substance should be had in school. The frame for it is found in different branches of study commonly taught which might inclose and organically connect elementary, ethical, economical, social and technical notions and ideas. In instruction in *religion* we may be sure of moral comprehension as well as moral effect, if we do not teach dogmatically, but show directly the influence of divine life upon human life; that is to say, place the facts of conscience, of charity, of joy in the good, etc., in the center of school life, and show their effect in the life of the child, in the life of the world which surrounds it; teach the child to feel the eye of God in every moment of its life. In *history* we can practice both the intellect and the moral will-power, by making the pupils familiar with the events and conditions of civilization in past and present, and making them see or comprehend the things as in a bird's-eye view in which each appears in its true relation to others; by awakening a clear insight into the facts that everywhere in the end the great moral ideas are victorious. In instruction in *German*, finally, the best opportunity is offered to discuss all that without restraint, connecting it with the ideals of our great poets.

Thus the school will teach how to grasp and understand life, by rising upon a higher level from which the ethical can be viewed without obstruction. Hence it would seem to me essential to make instruction in religion, history, and the mother tongue, the centers of the course of study and the daily practice.* That which is human and moral is thus placed into the center of the various ideas awakened by daily instruction; both mind and heart are formed in contact with it; intellectual power and moral character are both fed by it, and thus again, as so often, idealism "hits the center." For if we develop the power to think, and the moral

---

* This theory seems to me equally well adapted for boys' schools; I acknowledge, that it may not be realized there soon, these schools being, as it were, shaped by outer circumstances; but in our girls' schools we do not have to fear anything that might hinder us in the application of purely pedagogical principles.

character, we train much better for actual life than if we fill the head with sterile, positive knowledge. At this latter procedure Macé's fairy-tale is really aimed. Positive knowledge comes by itself, since we deal with positive material alone; thinking is learned from facts alone. These, however, will be retained better, and if lost regained more easily, if they are comprehended in connection with one another, if worked by independent mental activity into a homogeneous whole; indeed, vastly better are they retained than when they are offered in fragments, or detached bits, and imposed upon a mind that does not desire them.

But here is the difficulty. It is infinitely more difficult to find teachers who are able to thus conduct the ethical branches, than to find them for mere or purely intellectual branches, such as natural history and science, mathematics and foreign languages. To teach these latter branches a good head is necessary, while for the former a thoroughly cultured and harmoniously developed person is needed. Many teachers to whom are intrusted the ethical branches do not know what to do with them. In many schools, girls' as well as boys' schools, dogmatic religion is taught, and philological nonsense during the lessons in language; history here consists of cramming facts and cut and dried opinions into the memory. Indeed, such teaching is worse than none at all, for both mind and heart suffer under it, the moral sense is left dormant and the intellect is blunted; the mind is thus accustomed to play with formulas which later on are positive obstacles for independent judgment. Whatever else may be its faults, a real intellectual training would escape such jugglery.

Another more important reason is advanced in opposition to the emphasis given the ethical and in favor of purely intellectual branches. The ethical branches exercise a most powerful influence upon the development of character. A strong individuality—and only such a one influences pupils—will always impress its own views and opinions in religion, history, and poetry, despite all its efforts at objectivity; hence will influence children even more strongly and more lastingly than home or parents. How many fathers and mothers must feel that the spiritual life of their children is withdrawn from their influence, especially during the later years of the school course! Wherever the strength of a system is there also is its weakness. This suggesting of thoughts and awakening of impulses in school, it is very obvious, may be a blessing to the entire nation; it may also be a curse. The recognition of this fact has given rise to the movement of abolishing instruction in religion in the schools, and this only enables us to understand it.

But this example also points out the real cause of a possible danger. It can only arise when endeavors are made to lead ethical instruction in school toward a certain direction by decrees and regulations, combined with a system of promotions and official slights tending to secure that direction. The history of public education has recorded such periods; one of them is still vividly remembered. If in this way free spirit is fettered, ethical instruction is made to serve special purposes; if it is obliged to accomodate itself to the vacillations and ever-changing views of the ruling powers, if sentiments are to be made uniform and to be licensed, then, indeed, a system which pays exclusive attention to the intellectual branches would be preferable. But the other system is dangerous only in the case mentioned. If a certain liberty is granted to individuality, there will never be any real danger. Individualities always stimulate; they alone can draw heart to heart, because they have heart themselves. The one-sidedness of one individuality is offset by that of another. The pupil feels all through his school-life that he has contact with human beings, men with a spiritual life peculiarly their own, men of holy convictions, not merely figure-heads and puppets. A school system can rise only with outspoken individuality; it can remain on its height only when respecting individuality. It is a gratifying sign of the increasing consideration which the necessity of independence and individual importance finds in modern times when we see that even in military circles the spirit of the leaders is liberated by the abolishment of rigid forms, and thus made capable of self-active decision, that even for the private soldier close connection with others in columns is not advised any longer. Everywhere we see the tendency toward independent self-action. How much more is that necessity desirable in a school system where the justifiable individuality of independent minds should have free play, in order to secure the greatest possible effect. It should, at last, be comperhended that "a scattered line" in the great battle culture is fighting is preferable to "a closed line"; uniformity in scientific accomplishments is thereby as little endangered as the uniform technical training of the soldiers.

It seems to me very desirable to give into the hands of the pupil a weapon which enables him in ever-increasing individuality to meet his teacher; his mind must be liberated, so that he may acquire a control, as it were, a judgment, of what the teacher says; *jurare in verba magistri* (swearing by the word of the teacher) must be prevented. That is done best by thorough, formative training by means of the intellectual branches of study. But to place them in the center of instruction is not advisable, because they engender a certain coldness of heart and foster an egotism which is incapable of genuine enthusiasm. True and thorough culture is always caused through contemplation of humanity and life; if in combination with that the natural sciences receive due attention (since spiritual life can only be comprehended in connection with physical life, and man only in connection with nature) it would give, in my opinion, *genuine humanities*. That such a system *may* do injury does not lessen the truth of the principles upon which it rests, for every system may be abused. Nor is the fact that it will have good results only in the hands of good teachers of great weight; for though there are few Gertrudes, yet Pestalozzi's thoughts are unassailable.

This humane culture, offered to boys chiefly by men, to girls chiefly by women, would be my ideal of school education. Because the ethical branches have great power over the emotions and an absolute influence upon the development of character, I claim them for female teachers in girls' schools. That but few female teachers as yet understand the importance of these branches may be seen from the naïve astonishment expressed among them at my choice.

If we compare the German and the English girls' schools, it is seen that *we* lay more stress upon the *ethical*, the *Englishmen* more upon *intellectual* education. Both may have gone a little into excess, but, take all in all, I prefer our side. To prove the value of the German system in its results is perhaps impossible, from the fact that it has not had a proper chance to show its results. And, in fact, it seems to me doubtful whether the proof can ever be furnished. Who will trace the subtle threads that unite to cause a moral result? Human beings can not be furnished to order after models. Individuality and environments will decide whether the seeds we sow will take root. Regardless of that we must work on, the result, an average result, will not be wanting, though it be not always tangible. Ethical culture belongs to the imponderable fluids.

Such an instruction as our " German " * can be only rarely found in English high schools (where, of course, it would be called " English "), at least not

---

* Of course, the authoress means instruction in language and literature.

so extended and with such clear comprehension of what is aimed at. The fact that our literature is better suited for the purpose than the English may serve as an excuse. There is no literature in the world so suitable for ethical effect, and so pure and noble that its masterpieces may without hesitation be placed in the hands of children, as the German. It would be a difficult task to select or compile from English literature (not to mention the French) a canon of poetical works that offered suitable matter for instruction. English literature contains little or nothing that could be compared in variety, purity, and depth of effect upon a mind and heart just growing into self-consciousness with Schiller's and Uhland's poems, or anything that could in the least be compared in adaptability with Hermann und Dorothea, Iphigenie, Tasso, Jungfrau von Orleans, Nathan der Weise, etc.

Despite this great advantage, the matter should be sifted properly. True, we have instruction in religion (though in many schools only as a special study), but side by side with this study directly appealing to the heart should go another instruction, the object of which is to aim at the same truths in a roundabout way through the intellect. This is not found in English schools—neither in girls' nor in boys' schools—but the want is actually felt, and means are sought to supply it. A pamphlet by E. A. Manning on Moral Teaching in Schools points to that want and proposes an elementary course in ethics as a remedy; if that remedy were applied, we should still have an advantage in our instruction in "German" (provided it be well given) because it offers, unnoticed and as a matter of course, linked with exalted and noble personages, what such a course in ethics could only offer systematically and, as it were, intentionally. Perhaps by drawing more upon prose literature than is necessary with us a literary center may be found around which ethical instruction could be grouped.

The want of the English school system spoken of is met with, to a great extent, by some features of domestic and social life in England which are powerful enough to counteract the disadvantages arising from too great leniency during infancy. First, an excellent literature for children; second, systematic practice in charity from earliest childhood up. To this may be added an innate love of truth and a decisive energy of will-power.

I will touch upon these points but briefly. If our classic literature is incomparably better for ethical application in youth than the English it must be admitted that the English literature of fiction is superior for children and especially for young ladies.

It is represented by Miss Yonge, Maria Edgeworth, Louisa Charlesworth, Florence Montgomery, Miss Sewell, and many others; our Clara Cron, Clementine Helm, and whatever their names may be, are beaten from the field by the English. We have really only one who might equal the English authoresses, Ottilie Wildermuth, with her, at times, a little too sober view of life. Generally speaking, our literature is suffering from the fact that it introduces young girls into an unreal world; it describes to them the delights of the ball-room, of socials, teas and calls, etc., in bright but borrowed colors, and does everything to awaken emotions which had better lie dormant a few years longer. The English authoresses put before their young readers psychical problems suitable for their age and induce them to think about them; they picture the world as it really appears, but from the standpoint of a person who is working at his own development in all seriousness. These books (and English children read a great deal) partly take the place of our instruction in "German;" they induce to contemplation of self and give impetus to moral will-power through the channel of emotion.

English children generally have more chances for practical application of charity than ours. They learn human misery and need from observation;

they are early trained to place their strength into the service of charity. Active assistance of the poor and the sick belongs to the duties of which every English woman is conscious, and to the fulfillment of which she trains her daughters. As a particularly pleasing feature of some London high schools may be mentioned that in them "young ladies' associations" have been formed, the avowed object of which is to alleviate human misery; nowhere is misery shown so bare and undisguised as in London.

Thus home and practical life adjusts what is wrong in school. But that is no reason why the schools themselves should not do what is necessary. The great interest shown among the leading English women makes it reasonable to suppose that it will be done ere long.

CHAPTER VI.

INTELLECTUAL EDUCATION IN ENGLAND AND GERMANY.

WHILE I am sure that the English schools might borrow from Germany in regard to ethical education, the German schools might be induced to borrow from England in the matter of intellectual education. That the German girls' schools are not doing in this direction what may justly be expected has come to my knowledge, not through my own experience, but through statements made officially by men who have had much experience in examining young ladies. The consensus of their opinion is: Good solid knowledge in literature, history, and modern languages found frequently; but the efforts in composition less than mediocre, and the capacity for independent logical thinking below par. He who has had something to do with young ladies will know how difficult it is to make them think; yet we find that they did think when in the primary and grammar grades—yes, think well and much; but when they reach the upper grades a certain intellectual lameness becomes noticeable. That may be owing to the fact that the intellect (I don't mean the memory) is not sufficiently exerted. The old branches are gone over again; they do not call for much exertion, hence it would seem advisable to bring them into contact with an entirely new matter of thought during the years in which they are apt to become languid, so as to spur them to energetic action. What branch should that be? The English high schools offer the ancient languages and higher mathematics.

The ancient languages are taught in English girls' schools, as is well known, not on account of their ethical but simply on account of their intellectual importance. It is not expected that a pupil who stumbles through the ancient classics in the original will be filled with antique ideas and emotions, but the value of the study is found, or sought at least, in the mental gymnastics it offers. It would not be in place here to enter into the discussion that is now going on in Germany and in England with reference to the formative value of the ancient languages. I refer the reader to a book of recent origin—one of the best that has appeared on that subject, namely, Clemens Nohl's Paedagogik, respecting his arguments for the "middle school without Latin." I beg leave to say that I agree with every word he says. Public opinion, too, is more and more emphatic against the lofty airs which the classical high school (gymnasium) respecting the ancient languages assumes. It is no longer questioned that the mental gymnastics, thought possible only through them, are sought and found of late in other ways, and would generally be so acquired if it were not for the fact that the Government's favors are bestowed upon the graduates of classical schools. Certainly the formative value of the study of the classical languages is great; but modern life demands too much to spend the best years in training our mental faculties with means which, in themselves, have nothing to do with the actualities of life, and, besides, cause an overburdening which plays havoc with youth. My personal view of this is that a lessening of the great burdens of school, which seems so urgently necessary, can only be effected by limiting the extent of language instruction. It seems to me more than probable that the time is not very distant in which instruction in ancient languages will be greatly limited and the elements of modern languages acquired more rapidly than is done now (probably by means of improved methods, such as the "natural method," and by speaking these languages with teachers who have spent some time in foreign countries), in order to use these languages for the purpose of learning the life of other nations, their aspirations, views of life, and results of thought. Then the true value of linguistic culture, namely, ability to view a broader current of thought than is found in one's own nation, may be acquired; and then, too, the study of foreign tongues will aid in ethical culture, but not until then. A method which will make this possible with *children* is only applicable to living languages, because in them alone conversation is possible, and comprehension of the live present in contradistinction to the dead past.

The formative culture of language study, of which so much is said, will certainly be facilitated if many grammatical gymnastics that are now practiced before the language is known are limited to essentials. Grammar should follow and not accompany the acquisition of any language—at least, it should not begin until material enough is gathered from which to derive rules. ("Pupils should learn to think *in* a language before they are called upon to think *about* it."—Panitz.) In girls' schools, where, with regard to the choice of languages, more freedom is granted than in boys' schools, an early attention to this question is requested. Here reading and the live spoken word should take precedence of the grammar.

Hence it is obvious that I am opposed to the ancient languages in girls' schools. Their introduction into girls' schools in England is owing to the influence of men (the examining boards), partly also owing to time-honored custom. Not only Lady Jane Grey read Plato; the study of the ancients has never been neglected by the female sex in England. Though it may not have been pursued in boarding schools, it certainly has been privately. And then very obvious causes spoke too plainly to admit of disregard—I mean that, for admission into the colleges, a thorough preparation in the ancient classics was *conditio sine qua non*.*
Such reasons might, with almost equal force, be

---

* The views which I have here advanced are shared by many of the leaders of the English movement for the improvement of higher learning for women. They, however, acquiesced under the heavy pressure of circumstances. In England the opposition to the supremacy of the ancient languages in school is fully as strong as it is in Germany; and, if I am not very much mistaken, the years, if not the days, are counted after which those dead languages will not be *conditio sine qua non* of higher studies. When that takes place, the ancient languages in English high-schools will have to take a back seat, though they may not entirely be eliminated; and that will also be the case in women's colleges. That is the outspoken desire of such women as Miss Clough and Mrs. Sidgwick, I know. They have thus far only yielded to the, alas! strong argument: "We must learn as the men learn, or they will not recognize us."

advanced in Germany as long as the supremacy of the ancient languages continues. Many a mother would be delighted to be able to help her sons in their school work, and a little knowledge of Latin seems almost indispensable, considering the fact that Latin has so largely saturated scientific works. Hence, if the upper grade of our girls' schools (the so-called "selecta" class) would offer Latin besides other studies, no one would be apt to object. It is a wonder that it has not been done before, instead of the much less useful Italian taught in that class in some schools.

A thorough knowledge of the classic languages, I am well aware, is obligatory for the learned professions; but for those young ladies who would enter a foreign university — German universities admit no women—to prepare themselves for the learned professions, no opportunity offers itself for acquiring the ancient languages save private instruction. There, it seems to me, a remedy must be applied. But just as opposed as I am to change our girls' schools to classical schools, just as heartily am I in favor of establishing at least a certain number of classical schools for girls, so as to give those who intend to enter the university an opportunity to fit themselves for it. It would be fully early enough if they entered such a classical school when fourteen years old. They would then be old enough to judge of their own capabilities, old enough to know what they need for their future calling. Many would enter such a school even later, with mature mental powers, and would acquire the prescribed languages faster and with much less loss of time than is done in the proverbial classical schools of to-day. Thus, as special schools, these girls' "gymnasiums" or "real-schulen" would seem justified, and their establishment should be assisted by women all the more, since, according to the experiments made thus far, there is no other way open than self-help—at least, the state is not likely to lend a helping hand in the near future.

But back to the girls' schools, our text.

Although I should not recommend the introduction of the classical languages into the girls' schools (except, as stated, into special classical schools), because a very small percentage of the number of students would be benefited by them, I should with much emphasis urge the introduction of the *natural sciences* and *higher mathematics*. Natural sciences are taught in them now, it is true; but I should like to see them taught less like play and more in a manner which appeals to original thought. They would then be more like culture-studies. I have spoken of the *rôle* they must play as necessary complements to the ethical branches, namely, as a completion to the very desirable knowledge of life; I should now add, they are of enormous value as formative studies. The student learns in them correct observation of actuality, learns that she can approach truth only "through quiet and slow progress, leaning upon well-understood facts." More desirable than these studies even seems to me *mathematics;* I do not only regard it higher than language study as a formative study—the unrelenting logic with which a hasty conclusion is prevented is an irreplaceable means of education—but it offers exactly what we need to meet the want spoken of before—a new, hence interesting and elevating subject. I own willingly that it was only through experience that I renounced the prejudice I possessed against mathematics, thinking it an inadmissible study in girls' schools. Mathematics is taught with great zeal in English high schools, and the young ladies seem to express a preference for it by attempting the very difficult mathematical tripos in the university which presupposes very accurate and minute knowledge. The results of the high schools in mathematics, as stated by Schoell (Schmidt's Encyclopædia, Vol. iii, p. 1132) are thorough and good, and the examination rolls of the universities prove that even in higher mathematics very satisfactory results are accomplished. I believe it would be promoting the education of our girls, their practice in thinking and judging, if mathematics should receive a few more hours per week than are now given to it. These hours may be taken from other branches of less weight. If the languages were bled a little it might, perhaps, lead to better results, provided, of course, the ethical branches did not suffer by favoring the intellectual ones. I find that in this I am in accord with Clemens Nohl, who asserts that the doctrine that girls should be kept away from arithmetic and mathematics " is one of the numerous pedagogical dogmas which were invented by theorizers and thoughtlessly repeated by otherwise practical men—a dogma which one rationally conducted lesson in arithmetic or mathematics in any girls' school would completely upset." He desires these branches, in order to counteract the "sentimental, exuberant, fanciful twaddle" found there, tolerated and flourishing under the guise of "nourishment for the heart."

The sum total of my opinion concerning the woman question and female education in England is this: There are three causes that have led to a happy solution of the woman question: (1) The undisturbed, resolute, close union of English women without parties and factions; (2) the generous assistance of noble men; (3) the fact that the women not only demanded equal rights with men, but demanded the same accomplishments for themselves. That is what may serve us in Germany as an example. That the English women had at their disposal great funds, I consider of minor importance; these extensive means are simply in proportion to the entire English institutions; and so will our means be in proportion to *our* institutions and national wealth. Our men have a highly developed system of higher education, and the women could have the same if they wanted it; that is to say, if the same interest were awakened which I found in England.

And as to their advanced girls' schools, the English have this advantage—they concede to woman a wholesome influence in their management. The special emphasis which is bestowed in England upon exclusive intellectual, at the expense of ethical, culture does not meet my approval. But it must be admitted that England shares that preference with all other foreign nations. And yet I would not introduce the ancient languages, but would introduce mathematics as an intellectual branch in our girls' schools, and at the same time recommend the establishment of special classical schools for girls to accomodate the ever-growing number of young women who wish to prepare themselves for university studies.

It is admitted, as a matter of self-evidence, that the English system of female education is open to criticism and offers room for improvement; this is willingly admitted by English women. Perfection can not be reached in a single bound. But it is delightful to know that women were among the first who denounced the well-known mechanical drill in English schools. Boys' high schools, both public and private, are suffering under this senseless procedure, and the public lower schools seem to be doomed under the influence of machine regulations. It is confidently expected that the women will continue in the work of reform, and that they will in time to come do away with all the remnants of the old system. The absolute liberty of development enjoyed by the English system of higher female education makes easy a correction of errors and antiquated institutions when a resolute will employs its energy to that end. And the energetic initiative and great mental mobility shown by English women in starting the enormous school reforms will secure for their work a prospering future, despite all mistakes that may have been made in the beginning. For Germans the opinion of our celebrated countryman, Prof. Max Müller, of Oxford, may be of weight. To his initiative may be traced the establishment of a high school in Oxford. He pays a high tribute to the work done in it by women.

CHAPTER VII.

IN OTHER COUNTRIES OF EUROPE.

Whenever the possibility of admitting women to the German universities is discussed and the example of England is pointed out, it is replied that the circumstances are different and that a parallel can not be drawn. This answer seems very plausible, yet it is directed at a supposition which no one has made. No one is so foolish as to propose that the English institutions be transferred to Germany and servilely copied there. That I personally am not of that opinion is, I believe, clearly stated in the preceding pages, excepting a few things which are worthy of imitation. But what should be transplanted is the *principle* that to women should be opened the same studies, to them should be offered the same relief and the same encouragement that men enjoy. If this principle is once accepted, things will develop in Germany in a German manner, as they developed in England in an English manner.

Most European countries (not to speak of America) have either carried out this principle—at least with regard to university studies—or are beginning to do so. Let us see what is being done in other countries.

France.—This country began early to provide for the women in a most generous way. From 1866 till 1882 one hundred and nine academic degrees have been conferred upon women. Neither did the medical faculty raise any difficulties. The prejudice that the female intellect was not able to cope with the study of medicine was quickly overcome. With great candor, Ernest Legouvé, formerly an opponent of the cause, admits that he has been in error if he thought women incapable of pursuing scientific studies. In France there were no preparatory schools for the university. Only after the downfall of the second empire, after the humiliating experiences in 1870-'71, steps were taken favorable to women; the Government became convinced of the fact that an elevation of the whole people is only possible by means of an elevation of its women. The motion of Camille Sée to found and maintain lyceums for women was adopted without delay. "Our law is a moral as well as a social and political law," thus he pleaded for it, in 1880, before the Chamber of Deputies; "it concerns the future and security of France, for upon the women depends the greatness or decay of the nations."

Public opinion in France was favorable to Sée's law. The city of Rouen was the first that opened a lyceum for girls. It cost a million francs to build. One half of the expense was defrayed by the state, the other half by the community On the day on which the school was opened two hundred and two pupils were enrolled. In 1882 the state voted for an additional ten million francs for the establishment of such schools, and their number has since greatly increased.*

England.—The foregoing pages report fully what has been done in England. Ever since 1867 one privilege after another has been yielded, one college after another has been opened, and the number of women pursuing university studies has increased from five to as many hundreds.

---

* At present, January, 1890, France has fifty-one girls' lyceums (that is, high schools, to use an American term). Our sources of information differ as to the date and plan of the first girls' lyceum opened in France; some say the city of Montpellier was the first, others Rouen—the fact is immaterial, though. The last one opened is in Paris; it has cost two million francs, has six male and sixteen female teachers; the pupils are between seven and seventeen years of age. Besides the high-school branches, sewing and domestic economy are taught. The pupils who go through a post-graduate course of one year receive a teacher's license.—TRANSLATOR.

Switzerland. — As is well known, Switzerland opened its universities to women very early. Zürich was the first, in 1868; then followed Geneva, Bern, and Neufchâtel. The women here, like the women in England and France, have to do the same duties, but they enjoy also the same rights and privileges that the men have in regard to higher education.

Sweden. — Then followed Sweden, throwing open the doors of its universities to women. In 1870 they were admitted, and since 1873 they can acquire the same degrees in the arts and in medicine as are conferred upon men. The exemplary conduct of the young men toward the women in the universities of Sweden is justly commented upon.

Denmark followed in 1875. It opened its only university, that in Copenhagen. Women there may acquire all the degrees open to men save that of D. D., for the theological faculty is closed to them.

Italy.—In Italy the better-educated class has been favorable to the question of higher education of women. The Minister of Public Instruction, Bonghi, opened the university to women shortly before he was obliged to resign (1876).

Russia.—In 1867 the women petitioned the Government for admission to the universities, but Minister Tolstoi refused to grant it. Then the professors of the University of St. Petersburg made use of their right to give public lectures in such a way that they arranged complete courses, so that women were enabled to pursue university studies and prepare for examinations for ten years before they were officially admitted to the university. The same minister who had in 1867 refused to grant admission, at last, in 1878, agreed to having courses arranged for women in the University of St. Petersburg. They were attended quite numerously. The universities in Moscow, Kiev, Kasan, and others followed. *Finland*, as is well known, is ahead of other nations in this, as in many other educational movements.

Holland.—In 1880 the first female student was enrolled in the University of Amsterdam. In one respect Holland is ahead of all other countries, inasmuch as women there have never been debarred from admission to the university. The new law, passed in 1876, needed not have given women the right which, in fact, had never been denied them. They now certainly have the same right to matriculation and degrees that is offered to men, provided they pass the required examinations. The first enrollment of a woman in Amsterdam took place in 1880, but women had been studying in Groningen before that date. Now women are studying in all the four Dutch universities—Leyden, Utrecht, Groningen, and Amsterdam—though, as yet, their number is small.

Belgium.—In this country the first woman was admitted to a university course in 1881 (in Brussels). Since 1883 the admission of women has become general, and they are studying with good success in Brussels, Lüttich, and Ghent.

Norway.—Here the first woman, Miss Cecile Thoresen, asked to be admitted to the University of Christiania in 1880. According to the status and the charter of the institution she had to be refused admittance; but no sooner had this become known to the world than a member of Parliament proposed a bill to admit women to the *examen artium* and the *examen philosophicum*. The parliamentary Committee on Education reported the bill unanimously to the house, and in the two houses the bill was passed with a single dissenting vote. It became a law on July 15, 1882. When Miss Thoresen was enrolled, the students, who had always been favorable to the movement, sent her an address of congratulation and welcome.

About the state of affairs in *Spain* and *Portugal* I received, from trustworthy sources, the following information: There is no law in either of these countries which refuses women admission to the universities or any other public seats of learning, either as teachers or as pupils. The statutes and charters say nothing on that point. Hence, when women ask to be admitted no one refuses. However, the general idea is—and a justified one it appears—that the southern women have not the desire nor the intellectual and physical powers for scientific activity. Still, exceptions are appreciated without hesitation, and they are treated with true liberality and perfect courtesy. The names of such ladies are often quoted with admiration, but their example finds little imitation. The actual participation in academic studies is very small. A few women study at Madrid, Valladolid, and Barcelona, chiefly medicine. The Portuguese university at Coïmbra has never been asked to admit women, but in the medical school at Oporto three young ladies are enrolled. They have been studying with success for some years, and have regularly attended the "anatomy" classes (dissecting-rooms and clinics). Though university study is still considered an exception for women, the examinations arranged for elementary and high schools, to which, without exception, every boy and girl is admitted regardless of where and in what manner he or she acquired the knowledge asked for, are readily participated in by both sexes. These examinations have been held during the last six years. Hundreds of young ladies submit to them. The question of establishing special girls' lyceums is being agitated; a violent controversy has been going on concerning this, and the desire of many Portuguese is "that their ladies may remain in future as charmingly amiable and foolish children as they have been since Adam's time."

Of great nations in Europe there remain *Germany*, *Austria-Hungary*, and *Turkey*.

German Austria has at least made a beginning. A decree of the Minister of Education (in 1878) admits women to certain regular lecture courses of the university. Each case, however, is to be examined separately, and the decision as to whether an admission is to be granted is left to the college of professors, and particularly to that of the professor whose lectures are applied for. Enrollment, hence participation in working for a degree, is prohibited. It is obvious that this decree may mean much or little; it all depends upon the professors, whether they are favorable to the admission of women or not. In Vienna the professors have shown great willingness. The women studying there praise the consideration shown them by the professors and the excellent reserved conduct of the students. Here, then, is a case where the women have to fulfill all the duties imposed upon the men but do not enjoy their prerogatives. That they, for instance, have passed their examination for graduation is not given in documentary evidence; only privately the professors give a testimonial to that effect. Neither is their college register kept, and a private statement of their regular attendance is all they have hitherto been able to obtain. Nevertheless, their admission, limited as it is, is considered of value, since their attendance in Vienna is taken as "*prima facie* evidence" in other universities, such as Zürich. It is devoutly to be hoped that the Austrian Government will change this state of affairs and legalize it.

In *Hungary* three women have made an attempt to obtain admission to the universities of Buda-Pesth and Klausenburg. The university authorities were inclined to admit them, representing the principle: " Whoever proves that he possesses the required preparation is admitted to matriculation and the examinations of the university; sex is not considered." But the Minister of Culture, Trefort, refused his assent. Since this official died during the year 1889, it is reasonable to suppose that Hungary will not long lag behind in the great onward march of civilization, and then the German women will be the only ones in Europe—we need not take the women on the Balkan peninsula into consideration —who are excluded from university study.

CHAPTER VIII.

WHY WOMEN SHOULD BE ADMITTED TO UNIVERSITIES.

Attempts have also been made by women in Germany during the last two decades to obtain admission to the universities, though they were but rare cases. A few professors have looked upon such endeavors with favor, but they did not care to make themselves the leaders of the cause. Here and there admission has been granted to a few courses of lectures—especially to foreign ladies—but of late this has been surrounded by many limitations. The women are excluded on principle from passing the examination for graduation; not even a private examination is allowed them. The German women have to go to foreign countries if they will not forego a higher education.

It can not be asserted, and it certainly is not, that the two great nations of the German tongue have taken a very advanced position in this question, but German Austria stands ahead of Germany, to be sure.

To answer the question, why women insist at present upon admission to the university, is to give all the reasons for the great woman movement. In our time material and intellectual wants urge woman as never before. Material wants—the liberation of hand labor by machine labor, and the increasing tendency of men to remain unmarried, leaves a great number of women without visible means of support. The same circumstances create an intellectual want in circles where pecuniary aid is not needed, and this want is equally hard to bear. No one has described this more vividly than Miss E. Davies.

"Many fathers are no doubt aware that their daughters have very little to do. But that seems to them anything but a hardship. They wish they had a little less to do themselves, and can imagine all sorts of interesting pursuits to which they would betake themselves if they only had a little more leisure. Ladies, it may be said, have their choice, and they must evidently prefer idleness, or they would find something to do. If this means that half-educated young women do not choose steady work when they have no inducement whatever to overcome natural indolence, it is no doubt true. Women are no stronger minded than men, and a commonplace young woman can no more work steadily without motive or discipline than a commonplace young man. . . . People who have not been brought into intimate converse with young women have little idea of the extent to which they suffer from perplexities of conscience. 'The discontent of the modern girl' is not mere idle self-torture. Busy men and women—and people with disciplined minds—can only, by a certain strain of the imagination, conceive the situation. If they at all entered into it, they could not have the heart to talk as they do. For the case of the modern girl is peculiarly hard in this, that she has fallen upon an age in which idleness is accounted disgraceful. The social atmosphere rings with exhortations to act, act in the living present. Everywhere we hear that true happiness is to be found in work—that there can be no leisure without toil—that people who do nothing are unfruitful fig trees which cumber the ground. And in this atmosphere the modern girl lives and breathes. She is not a stone, and she does not live underground. She hears people talk, she listens to sermons, she reads books. And in her reading she comes across such passages as the following: 'It is real pleasure to me to find that you are taking steadily to a profession, without which I scarcely see how a man can live honestly. That is, I use the term *profession* in rather a large sense, not as simply denoting certain callings which a man follows for his maintenance, but rather a definite field of duty, which the nobleman has as much as the tailor, but which he has not who, having an income large enough to keep him from starving, hangs about upon life, merely following his own caprices and fancies; *quod factu pessimum est.**

"Or, again, such a passage as this: 'Que de femmes, si vous exceptez les mères qui se donnent à leur famille, que de femmes, hélas, dont la vie se passe entière dans de futiles occupations, ou dans des conversations plus futiles encore! Et l'on s'étonne que, rongées d'ennui, elles recherchent avec frénésie toutes les distractions imaginables! Elles accusent la monotonie de leur existence d'être la cause de ce vague malaise; la vraie cause est ailleurs, elle est dans la fadeur intolérable, non d'une vie dépourvue d'événements et d'aventures, mais d'une vie dont on n'entrevoit pas la raison ni le but. On se sent vivre sans qu'on y soit pour quelque chose, et cette vie inconsciente, absurde, inspire un mécontentment trop fondé.' †

"Such things the modern girl reads, and every word is confirmed by her own experience. . . . She

---

* Letter to Dr. Greenhill, an old pupil, in Life of Dr. Arnold, p. 392.

† Sermons par T. Colani, Deuxieme Recueil, p. 293.

seeks for counsel, and she finds it. She is bidden to 'look around her'—to do the duty that lies nearest. . . . She looks around her, and sees no particular call to active exertion. The duties that lie in the way are swallowed up by an energetic mother or elder sister. . . . She feels no sort of impulse to take up any particular pursuit or to follow out a course of study; and so long as she is quiet and amiable, and does not get out of health, nobody wants her to do anything. Her relations and friends—her world— are quite satisfied that she should 'hang about life, merely following her own' (or their own) 'caprices and fancies.' The advice given, so easy to offer, so hard to follow, presupposes exactly what is wanting—a formed and disciplined character, able to stand alone and to follow steadily a predetermined course without fear of punishment or hope of reward. Ought we to wonder that, in the great majority of cases, girls allow themselves to go drifting down the stream, despising themselves, but listlessly yielding to what seems to be their fate?

"An appeal to natural guides is most often either summarily dismissed or received with reproachful astonishment. It is considered a just cause of surprise and disappointment that well brought up girls, surrounded with all the comforts of home, should have a wish or a thought extend-

ing beyond its precincts. And perhaps it is only
natural that parents should be slow to encourage
their daughters in aspirations after any duties and
interests besides those of ministering to their comfort and pleasure. In taking for granted that this
is the only object, other than that of marriage, for
which women were created, they are but adopting
the received sentiment of society. No doubt, too,
they believe that in keeping their daughters to
themselves till they marry they are doing the best
thing for them as well as pleasing themselves. If
the daughters take a different view, parents think it
is because they are young and inexperienced, and
incompetent to judge. The fact is, it is the parents
who are inexperienced. Their youth was different
in a hundred ways from the youth of this generation; and the experience of thirty years ago is far
from being infallible in dealing with the difficulties
and perplexities of the present. No doubt, young
people are ignorant and want guidance. But they
should be helped and advised, not silenced. Parents
take upon themselves a heavy responsibility when
they hastily crush the longing after a larger and
more purposeful life."*

And that is done daily, not only in England, but

---

* The Higher Education of Women, by E. Davies, p. 47.

also in Germany. Who has the courage to say that the sympathetic description of Miss Davies does not fit our circumstances? Who is bold enough to assert that *every* young lady in our wealthy families can find sufficient occupation for her internal and external life if she but look for it? A number of them probably. There are families in which the daughters are sufficiently and satisfactorily occupied with domestic duties; there are other girls who without being really occupied are contented in beautifying the lives of their parents and friends of the family as welcome home-spirits until they marry; or, if they do not marry, they lead a happy, peaceful existence, full of blessing for others, as the ever welcome "aunties." But blissful such an existence is only when it is chosen voluntarily. If the girl who is to beautify life fights a battle royal with the desire to be of use, to create an existence of her own, it would seem a downright sin committed upon undying reason to deny it to her, provided no real duty intercedes. Now, what kind of an existence is she to create for herself? That which she chooses. It stands to reason that not all these young girls can devote themselves to university studies; the word of charm against modern pessimism is not university culture, but *work*—useful, practical work generally. That the need of that is growing more and more is shown by the great number of female candidates crowding the examinations for teachers' certificates. And they are not all driven to it by material want, but a considerable number of them simply look for a firm discipline, a definite aim to work up to. Even the desolate memory work that is required of them by a series of examinations seems to be preferable to the utter emptiness of their existence, preferable also to amateur work, this intellectual nibbling and aimless listening to fashionable lectures. Complaint is raised about the crowds of female applicants at teachers' examinations, and they are interpreted as evil signs of the time. *There can be no better sign.* That a thing happens which in former times would have been thought outrageous, namely, that the daughters of our first families long for work, and demand rational, intelligent assistance in, and control of their studies, that they elevate the profession upon which they used to look down, may be, and should be, considered a gain which can not be gauged too high.

But the teacher's profession is not everybody's calling. Let them choose another. It is equally gratifying to notice that nursing the sick is beginning to be taken up as a profession and that it is deemed important enough to be learned professionally. Likewise it is a sign of better times that the kindergartens begin to attract the girls of better situated classes. The dominion of art industry also —yes, and trades—are opening to women. All that, however, is insufficient. If work is to have a redeeming influence, it must be chosen in conformity with one's taste. One must have the right to choose according to one's own powers and talents. Nobody chooses otherwise. Hence no field of labor should be denied, not even the highest intellectual labor. Those who intellectually hunger should be offered the best intellectual food available in Germany. No one should in Germany be denied opportunities to fill that inner desolate void, no one obliged to stifle what is considered the highest sign of superiority—a longing for serious mental and professional work. Yet this murder of the mind is committed daily in our country.

Should any one be impenetrable to such arguments for offering professional training and the professions themselves to women he may be open to practical ones. They are the ever increasing need of women and the necessity for employing them in certain professions. It is still customary to deny the need among German women. A few figures will prove it. According to the census of December 1, 1885, Germany had 15,181,823 adult women, that is, women of marriageable age, sixteen years and over. Of these, 7,944,445, or 52·3 per cent, were married; 5,155,241, or 34 per cent, were unmarried; 2,082,137, or 13·7 per cent, had been married. Hence, taking the last two numbers together, there were 7,237,378 women, or 47·7 per cent, without "natural supporter," leaving out of consideration the fact that many of those who had this supporter were still without support.

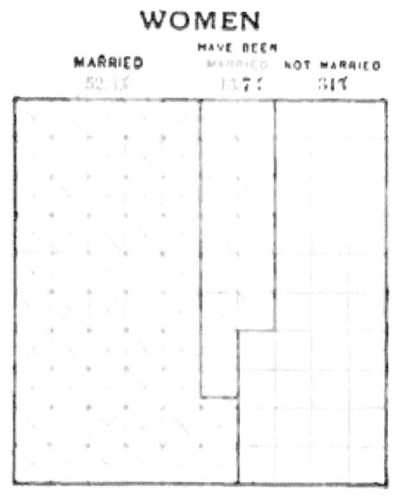

The number of unmarried women and widows who are not working for their support, or only indifferently, who either by family connection or in possession of a fortune of their own are in circumstances that shield them (if not from intellectual) from material want, that number I estimate at about two millions. Hence, leaving out of sight the number of women who work for the support of their families and thus aid the "natural supporter," there must be five million women, unmarried or widows, who temporarily or permanently earn their own living, and, in many cases, those dependent upon them. Now, as far as the lower strata of society are concerned, a part of them find occupation quite easily, partly in positions as servants occupied with purely female work, partly competing with men, with whom they stand in perfect equality, if not in wages, at least in regard to intellectual culture. Many of these have to toil inexpressibly, but they have at least the satisfaction that the men have no better lot than theirs. In these walks of life there are no arbitrarily made differences between man and woman. The woman question in the lower classes is therefore only an integral part of the great social problem. But in the middle and higher classes we meet an arbitrary disparity, hence, one that may easily be removed; and in these classes we meet most unmarried women. Here man has privileges; he has not only advantages given him by nature, but also advantages bestowed upon him by society, that is, by his own sex; and thus the weight of the misery, which may be supposed if we look at the foregoing figures, is doubled. He has all the opportunities for education, and all imaginable facilities. To woman is denied the state's sanction, even to an education acquired independently of state aid, except the professional education of a teacher. To him are open all the many places in the civil service, where a life-long maintenance is awaiting him; to women places are open to such limited extent that they almost disappear from sight.

And yet a cry of desperation is raised among the better educated classes, that is, among the ones who have fewest prospects, when their women make an attempt at participating in the privileges of man in order to acquire the knowledge made necessary for competition by the existing circumstances, and they are ever and again reminded of their "natural calling." Verily, he is not to be envied for his heart or his judgment who in the face of the foregoing figures still has the courage to point out to those who cry for bread or a satisfactory sphere of activity a calling which they are unable to follow. In the face of the foregoing figures such phrases as "natural calling" and the "position of woman as assistant of man" are cruelty. The statistical data, or ratios, mentioned are not essentially different from those in other countries; but everywhere a beginning is made in removing the separating barriers. The fate of women is made easier by opening all the professions, and thus offering at least a limited number of them a satisfactory maintenance. The greater physical and mental power of resistance man has, and his higher capacity for competition resulting therefrom will still leave the great majority of women in misery. I am at present concerned about the learned professions. It is obvious, then, that by opening them to only a limited number of women, a certain class only would be benefited. How the other classes might be benefited can be seen in France, England, Belgium, Switzerland, and in parts of southern Germany where women are employed in railroads, telegraph, telephone, and postal service. That in all these spheres talent and training must decide is a matter of course; but that talent and training should be found wanting in Prussian women is scarcely credible.

The necessity of having women in certain spheres of action where formerly they were not found has made itself felt chiefly in the medical profession. It is generally acknowledged that female physicians have become a necessity, owing to the phenomenal increase of female maladies. Yet, rarely does any one take the part of women to oppose those arguments of male physicians which are not always prompted by the purest of motives. These men, strange to say, have recently found an eloquent ally in Prof. Wilhelm Waldeyer, who, in the last congress of natural scientists at Cologne, gave utterance to a loud protest against the opening of the medical profession to women. I can not leave this protest unnoticed in view of the elevated position Waldeyer occupies, and because he touches some points of vital importance.

If Waldeyer intends to say that among the ancient civilized nations the position of women has been equally favorable with that of men, it needs better proofs than such examples furnish as the "hetaeri" of Greece, who participated in politics (*das politisirende Hetaerenthum*), or the women of the Roman empire. If *these* women knew no social barrier, other causes hindered them from accomplishing anything in art or science. Their sisters were incapable of rising because of mechanical drudgery or paralyzing oppression of unworthy dependence; but *they* were enervated by luxury, and had become incapable of intellectual initiative; they could at most only play coquettishly with intellectual questions. A double curse rested upon woman during ancient times—a mind-killing oppression of mechanical work, or else the enervating charm of voluptuous indolence. Woman was either a slave or an article of luxury. The woman of the middle ages, also, though she began to distinguish herself by more refined culture of the mind, and often found satisfaction in it, did not know the strongest incentives to intellectual work—neither the necessity of professional labor nor the feeling of outer and inner independence that has been developed so strongly in our time, nor even the intellectual need which is perceived more acutely now than during the middle ages—ages that had for material and for intellectual need an equally applicable panacea, the convent. Hence we are justified in saying, that only in our modern age have conditions arisen that enable woman to show what she can do.

But I admit that if in these women a great creative power had been alive they never would have tolerated the pressure of the unfavorable circumstances mentioned. I furthermore readily admit that, in comparing the intellectual talents of the two sexes, we find that creative power in much greater degree in man than in woman, hence, that science and art will till doomsday be promoted more by man than by woman. Waldeyer confronts this creative activity by woman's receptivity; but he entirely forgets that between them lies a third activity —the practical application of science and art. It may be possible that a woman rarely if ever essentially promotes science; but is that a reason why she should not practice it? If a line is to be drawn around the practice of learned professions where independent creative activity begins, it is reasonable to suppose that the women, with few exceptions, will stand outside of that line, *but also ninety per cent of the men.* If all the male physicians and teachers who are not capable of promoting science independently be excluded from their professions, nine tenths of mankind would not know to whom to apply for relief in case of sickness, or would not know to whom to appeal for education. Why the capability of independent scientific work should be made a criterion for the practitioner I fail to comprehend. A physician or a teacher who has the talent for original work is not unconditionally the best in his profession; he is apt to neglect his daily duties. The woman whose mental ability is, if not sufficient for essential promotion of science, at any rate fully sufficient for an independent practice of the physician's or teacher's profession will concentrate all her attention upon the practical application of her professional knowledge; and, if looked at from a disinterested standpoint, she ought to be welcomed, because she relieves man and liberates his powers for the further promotion of science; and if, as Waldeyer fears, the number of men devoting themselves to the medical profession will decrease if women gain admission to it, this could only be deplored in case men were actually superior to women in their practical skill also; but competition alone can prove it.

Prof. Waldeyer is right. "The mind is the

most terrible weapon of the human being." This sentence being true, I long to be able to see why the men constantly employ physical strength in order to keep women from the intellectual arena! If it is true "that in all cases in which man and woman in free competition enter any sphere of action woman is always defeated," why, then, move heaven and earth in order to keep her from being defeated? Why does Prof. Waldeyer call upon the authorities to protect the stronger sex against the weaker? It must be that there is something not quite right in the female brain; for not even the logic of such an argument is understood by it.

However, science is said to suffer when women enter the learned professions, and the men are not strong enough to keep it from harm! It is really a very fine psychological touch that makes Adam say, "The woman gave me of the tree and I did eat." The same thing is expressed by Max Nordau, in a preface which I dislike to see in the book of a woman; he says that the women are the cause of the degeneration of German literature—" the woman gave it to me and I did eat." The objection is scarcely to be taken in earnest.

In what Prof. Waldeyer next says of sexual differentiation and the division of labor resulting therefrom there is much truth. He draws the conclusion from it that woman had better stay within that sphere in which she possesses natural powers and capability for development. Exactly; but what sphere is that? Man decides that for her. Much is said of natural instincts. If at present the women demand in ever increasing numbers to have their share in the work of civilization, in the profession which the men have claimed for themselves, I think that this is instinct, a feeling or consciousness that their natural sphere is more extended than the one assigned to them hitherto. It is, in other words, a resentment of nature against those who intend to oppress it. The necessary division of labor does not seem to me to agree with the division of vocations of which Prof. Waldeyer speaks so plausibly. According to him, we women should have to claim a good deal more, because the vocations now all belong to men. Mrs. Weber calls attention to the fact that the Chinese in the United States already do laundry work; is that, perhaps, to be claimed by men as man's vocation? But we women are very tolerant; none of us protest against that. We modestly demand nothing else than that, *mutatis mutandis*, Lessing's questions regarding the preacher and the dramatist be applied: "May a man devote himself to woman's work? Why not, if he will? May a woman practice man's calling?

Why not, if she can?" So far as Nature dictates a division of vocations, we all agree. Mathilde Lammers is right when she says: "At the anvil I shall always imagine a man; at the cradle, always a woman." The inner household, the management of the family, are things which a woman will never give up; the outward defense of the peace of the house will always be assigned to the greater physical strength of the man. In this division there is nature; but not in the separation of intellectual and mechanical labor, of which the latter, though claiming a great amount of physical exertion, is willingly assigned to the wife; the former, as the more interesting, more satisfactory, and more lucrative, is claimed by the husband. Women have the same right to intellectual labor that the men have, and the differentiation of sexes will only partly be expressed in the division of vocations. It will partly be felt in the individual manner in which the same vocation is considered and practiced by the different sexes. If man, for instance, will bring to the profession of teaching greater acuteness of thought, better system, and greater power, the woman will furnish greater versatility, power of adaptation, and, above all, more patience. If both sexes participate, the profession can only gain by it; one sex will learn from the other. To this it is to be added, that in the profession of teaching and the medical profession the fact of there being two sexes in the human race is an additional cause for employing both; girls are better taught by women, boys by men, and many sick women want to be treated by women only.

Despite all objections that he raises, Prof. Waldeyer acknowledges that it is a serious task "to secure for women other conditions of existence"; he grants that the woman question deserves intense and permanent interest. But I fail to find in what other manner that interest should take effect, except in removing the barriers which prevent woman from creating her own "conditions of existence." That is the only way she can be helped. I believe that Prof. Waldeyer is serious in claiming a sympathy with the cause. He disdains, though an opponent of higher female education on principle, the many favorite and often-used exaggerations and misrepresentations, although he lays too much stress upon the opinion of some unchivalrous opponents of women. But search as carefully as I may, I can find no way in which the interest spoken of can be promoted, and, strange to say, he does not indicate any either. For the proposition he makes, to leave it to the professors to admit some specially talented women to their lectures, can scarcely be considered as seriously promoting the interests of women. A diploma of graduation is demanded of the man, not special talent. All men intend to earn their bread —those who are not specially talented as well as the rest, and they intend to secure it by means of diligence and average results. The same holds good with women. Why should exceptional conditions be imposed upon them?

But enough of this, and enough of the medical profession. Among the practical reasons why the universities should be opened to women may be counted the necessity to procure female teachers who are thoroughly versed in science.

How I personally regard the question, I have expressed emphatically enough. I should consider it a mistake if any university studies, especially philology, were made obligatory in the highest grade of girls' high schools. Though I have been convinced that the average woman (where hundreds study it will hardly do to speak of exceptions) is capable of pursuing scientific studies to a much higher degree than I had assumed at first, and though I have been convinced also that woman may preserve her womanliness in such a pursuit, I have nevertheless not changed my views. Every one knows that the English universities are not, like ours, special schools of the four faculties, but more like nurseries of general culture. On account of this character and owing to their less high aims, the English university is more suitable, according to my ideas, for preparing teachers who are not necessarily to be scholars. But such things are matters of opinion, and I can not expect to see the same kind of a bark grow on all trees. I, for my part, have wished and asked for the establishment of special institutions for female teachers in which their studies, without injury to thoroughness, are directed with reference to their future vocation. This motion has been rejected abruptly, without opening ways upon which the teachers might acquire the necessary professional education. Every attempt at realizing even partially the ideas mentioned before will be hailed with delight by me; thus, for instance, the establishment of professional courses in history and German in the Victoria Lyceum, which have been made possible through the warm interest which our Empress Frederick entertains for teachers.

But that is only a narrow foot-path which but few can walk in. If not any more broad and straight roads are to be built, if under sanction of the Government only these two branches are to be taught and in one city of Germany alone (mere private enterprise has not the least value for obvious reasons), it would seem unjust to refuse female teachers who can not walk this road permission to select another, even though it be a roundabout one. Hence, if they (as I have noticed repeatedly) have the desire to pursue a university study, believing that thereby they will find greater satisfaction for their own ambition, no one should hinder them in that. Since the authorities guarantee the women teachers in their certificates of examination the right to teach in the highest grades of school, the acquisition to this formal right is not dependent upon any definite university course, and hence the women may select whatever branches they see fit. I consider a mere university course unfit for the preparation of female teachers, and I am very decided in my belief that it would be attended by great dangers for our girls' schools if a university course were made obligatory. And yet the necessity for granting female teachers the opportunity to learn true science somewhere is so urgent that, in view of the hopelessness of seeing my own plans realized, I advocate this optional studying. If it is an evil, it is at least the smaller of two evils, and we are almost forced to choose it. After the explicit refusal of our certainly modest demands, the question arises: Shall our teachers again be condemned to elementary knowledge which precludes higher aspirations, or shall they at least have a possibility of higher studies after leaving the normal school? Shall they in this roundabout way attempt to acquire that practical and theoretical knowledge which should be combined by all means? In Zürich this way has been adopted for some time, and it is my opinion that it would be unjust to keep those who want to use it from doing so. It is confidently expected that scholarships will be granted in time, as has been done for students of medicine and the natural sciences. But I should raise my voice to warn against an overestimate of philological studies. A few years' sojourn in foreign countries is of more decided value, provided sufficient preparation has been had, than philological studies in a university; I mean for female teachers of the upper grades of girls' schools, because those studies in a university contain much that is totally unproductive for our girls' schools. Literary, historical, and scientific studies obtained in German universities could be recommended for female teachers, if—yes, if there was a Germany in which science was free for women also.

That many of my colleagues, as I have become aware of late, would rather take a course in a university than a course better fitted for themselves as well as for the subsequent application in school, is easily explained by the fact that man, upon whose opinion all these things hinge, will not consider a study worth much unless it is the same in kind with his. The course I have suggested may require, perhaps, the same exertion, the same sacrifices of time and money, without offering the same advantages that university study and university degrees possess. The future will judge these things differently. Meanwhile we have to reckon with arguments of this kind, and it will be owing to them if such arrangements as have been made in the Victoria Lyceum, gratifying as they may be, do not in time to come find the recognition and use which are desirable. Another unfortunate feature is this — the female teachers studying in the Berlin Victoria Lyceum have to teach during the day. If the authorities would here use some of their prerogatives to ease the burden of these teachers by giving them a leave of absence for a portion of the day, as is done in like cases with the male teachers, much would be done to make the experiment a success. As it is, it appears to me as though a beginner in the art of swimming is made to go into the water with a heavy load around his neck. But perhaps the prospect of a future and appropriate employment would make these women bear even this double burden. Woman, like man, dislikes to work in vain. But what is to be expected in this direction can best be expressed with Dante's words, "Ye who enter here leave all hope behind." It is not impossible that these circumstances make the courses offered in the Lyceum a gift from the Danai. If they prove a failure (*im Sande verlaufen*), it will be alleged that it proves a want of desire to learn on the part of woman, while, in fact, it would be attributable to other causes. Meanwhile, let us hope. It is a very favorable sign for our female teachers that they desire a higher education, and that they have, without any apparent prospect for promotion and in spite of being occupied all day with teaching, undertaken these higher studies. Let us wish and hope that their strength and courage will hold out to the end. If no other schools, then, at least the private schools will actively appreciate their efforts.

CHAPTER IX.

CAUSE OF FAILURE IN GERMANY.

We have now brought together sufficient material to proceed to a systematic reply to the question, Why is it that the women of Germany do not succeed in a cause in which the women of other civilized nations have succeeded? Do they have to look for the causes in themselves, or are the men the causes, or can it be accounted for by insurmountable obstacles?

For the purpose of arriving at a satisfactory answer, I will reverse the order of these three queries and begin with the third, for the unfavorable circumstances are invariably put into the foreground when we women point out that in other countries the woman question is about to be solved by granting them the requisite liberties and concessions. We are told that there are as yet a great many men to be provided for; but that is the case in other countries, also, where their sex does not give them so much of a preference as in Germany. I know full well that an inquiry for the reasons of this preference is thought very indiscreet. But to an unbiased mind it will ever seem odd that the strong man should find the protection of the government so much more readily than the weak woman, who, in the battle for subsistence, has such serious disadvantages that it would seem as though she deserved being taken care of first. Is man a human being of the first class, woman one of the second, in Germany? Or is it supposed that hunger and privation are less painful to woman? We are told the man deserves to be provided for first, because he has to provide for others. Yet I know of no woman earning her own living who does not support either her old parents, or brothers at school, or other needy members of her family. Hence the principle can not be applied against all women. And, in truth, it is not applicable at all; for the inference would be that married men—not only under like qualifications, where such a preference might be justified sometimes but at all times—would be preferred to unmarried ones; that the claim for support should rise in exact proportion to the number of children. In carrying out this principle, the salaries would be in proportion to the wealth of children, and every new arrival in the family would be the "cause of an increase of salary"; furthermore, that the salary should stand in inverse proportion to private income, and so forth. Who would advance such absurdities! But if one refuses to accept its consequences, the principle is of no account. Indeed, it is only held up against women. When men among themselves compete with one another one thing only is taken into consideration—the position is given to him who is the most capable. Why is not this extended over both sexes? And why is not the opportunity offered to women as well as to men to obtain the requirements wanting? There are evidently only two cases possible—either all men are more capable than all women (then the former have nothing to fear from the competition of the latter and could refute the women by granting their demands) *or* some women are more capable than some men; is it just in that case to keep the less capable men in positions that by right belong to the more capable women?

In short, I shall have to be satisfied with an answer to my question like that which I heard somebody give a little girl recently who complained that her brother had received a larger piece of cake than she: "Well, is not he a boy?" The answer had a silencing effect.

But let us further examine the conditions peculiarly German that are said to be always obstacles in the way of higher education of women. "The conditions that exist at our universities do not admit it." Why not? The examinations are more difficult than elsewhere. May be, but who asks that they should be made easier for women? The demand is that women be admitted under precisely the same conditions applied in the case of men. If the women prove less capable to come up to the requirements, as may probably be the case in the beginning, it could only please those who desire to limit the higher studies of women; but that the degree of difficulty of the examinations should be a cause for non-admittance of the woman is incomprehensible to me. Furthermore: "Our students would never tolerate females as fellow-students." Can we really be so far behind other nations in culture? But that leads me to a point that deserves a more extensive treatment.

It is true that the German student has yet many traits of the old university life (*vom alten Burschen*), still, I think, he has enough reverence for woman to respect her, even if he sees her walking unfamiliar roads, provided she remains a woman. But I do not require him to respect women to whom science is the subordinate, and the life of a student the principal object in view. I fear, in this respect, that much mischief has been done by foreign women in Switzerland, who have thus made the life of their successors, who are bent upon pursuing science, a life of many hardships. The cause of unwomanly excesses may be found in the fact that the young girls in the university often have no choice except to live as male students do without any restraint, to take their meals and to lodge without intimate association with older educated women. Of course, gradually but surely, the sense for that which is proper gets blunted, and the maxim "Allowed is what is proper" must yield to "Allowed is what pleases." I can suggest only one remedy, namely, the one that was applied in England, of course adapted to existing institutions. I mean the establishment of boarding institutions in which the students associate with older, finely educated women and are subject not to harsh discipline, but to moral influence; homes in which the student enjoys the same liberty that an educated and cultured lady *has*, or better, *takes* in her own home. For the liberty to lead a street or tavern life, which seems to be the highest ambition for a young man after entering the university, is one which a cultured woman will not take even where the circumstances would permit it. Since she can not find interesting society in taverns and on the street, she needs it all the more at home. A woman must not, during the years of study, lose the instincts which make her seek her happiness at home; she must not lose the standard of measurement for what she may or may not do. In time to come and under the influence of another kind of education she will be enabled to avoid breakers on which she is likely to experience shipwreck at present. Independent and happily organized natures may even now be able to manage their own affairs without danger for their future lives, but for the majority of German girls, raised as they mostly are, dependent upon others, a home like the English home-colleges (though less luxurious), with pleasant surroundings, musical evenings and teas, a little gentle discipline (for only such it must be), would be very welcome and useful. Many parents would be more willing to permit their daughters to satisfy their craving for higher studies, as Mrs. Weber sagely remarks, if it was not for the—blameless—living alone outside of the family circle.

As the young female students need confidential advice at home, so they need occasionally advice and aid in their studies. Both can not, as is the case with young men, be given by the professors. With less embarrassment and more confidence the young ladies would approach a woman for that purpose. It is reasonable to think that if a woman stood at the head of such an institution (as is the case in Girton College), a woman who knows the course of study pursued by the students and has been graduated herself, she would give wise counsel and active assistance better than men could. In University College, in London, a lady superintendent has an office in the building where she may be called upon by the young lady students who need advice and assistance. This has proved to be practical and effective, and does not lead to misunderstandings, since the conduct of the professors directs that of the students. There can be no objections to serious intellectual work done by women who live together, work done for a serious purpose. I leave out of consideration all who consider the pursuit of higher knowledge unwomanly, for I have no arguments to convince them. And I confidently believe that the male students of Germany would not treat the women improperly who thus come to be their fellow-students.

In short, it does not seem to lie in external circumstances that the women of Germany are not successful. Even pecuniary difficulties can not be advanced as causes of their signal failure. Germany is not so poor that it might not create facilities for higher education of women, since the existing institutions for men could mostly be shared.

Is it the men, then, who cause the signal failure? Without doubt they are partly the cause. For many years certain women have tried to interest men of influence in their cause, but it must be confessed, they have not found the reception that the women found among men in other countries. The year in which Girton College was founded, and the professors and students of Cambridge observed its growth with increasing interest, is the same year (1872) in which a teachers' congress at Weimar met with scorn and derision the women who advocated the plan of founding a modest academy for women. The propositions and petitions which subsequently were submitted to the authorities with reference to that plan were left wholly unnoticed. The authorities engaged men exclusively as principals in higher girls' schools, although women may be had who have through self-instruction gained the necessary requirements and have proved in private schools that they are capable of managing schools as well as teaching the higher branches. A motion emanating from the "Lette-Verein" to establish higher schools of learning for women was rejected; the German Woman's League, who made similar attempts, was equally unsuccessful, though they had such active women as Mrs. L. Otto-Peters, Mrs. A. Schmidt, and Mrs. H. Goldschmidt as spokeswomen. Wherever woman was given a trial in any branch it was done with ill-concealed distrust. She was watched suspiciously, and at the first signs of weakness or error the trial was pronounced a signal failure. Wherever women were busy in "man's callings" they found, if not direct malevolence, certainly not a hearty reception.

I am reporting a few facts only. It would be easy to enumerate many more. What is their cause? It would be unjust to account for them exclusively by man's ill-will and fear of competition, though these motives must be considered. A great number of men are indifferent; they never have thought about the woman question; they do not know the needs that have called the question into life. That they do not know them is to be charged to their wives. The wife should persuade the husband to support the cause of women. That cause generally lies remote from men's professional walks. What they hear of it are accidental disconnected fragments of the great discussion, so unsatisfactory that the men turn away from them disgusted, amused, or exasperated. It is interesting to observe that most of those who feel exasperated are among the most chivalrous of their sex. Even men with exalted views of women, men with ideas of her difficult natural calling and the duties it requires, turn with disgust from the proposition to set up a new order of things for the dear ones whom they are in duty bound to support or protect. I have often had occasion to notice that this chivalrous idea caused men to totally disregard the actual conditions under which woman lives, and particularly those numerous unfortunates who have no such knight, but are obliged to face the hard conditions of life single-handed, conditions that must be met. Every noble man can be convinced of his prejudices by logic and reference to existing facts, and he will be ready to yield to the right which he had unknowingly disregarded.

But there are other men to be considered, those who apply derision as the only answer to the woman question. "Scoffing ends where comprehension begins, says a psychologist. Indeed, mockery in this case can have no other origin than absolute ignorance. Every man with but half a conscience would be frightened if he knew the actual misery that has originated the woman question and become convinced that at the expense of such misery he had been entertaining his wit; that with his derision, which he had been using so victoriously, he had been killing a thousand possibilities that might have given bread to the hungry, happiness to the unfortunate—yes, even saved to honor those who are walking the ways of dishonor." *

---

* Familie and Individuum, by J. M. Frauenberuf, vol. ii.

If in England the men were better acquainted with the woman question, and hence erred less through ignorance, the cause of this may be found in their own wives who informed them of its bearings; generally, it may be said, the married women in England interested themselves in the question very actively. I shall certainly not attack German family life. It is distinguished from that of other nations in many features which I would not have otherwise, but it is more apt to make the women selfish; that is, it engenders family-mania—(*selbstsüchtig—oder richtiger familien-süchtig*). The life of a German housewife is so completely lost in her own interests and those of her family that she gives scarcely a thought, with some notable exceptions of course, to her sisters who stand outside, literally starving intellectually and wildly groping for a life's sustenance. She neglects to enlist her husband for the fight which the women can undertake and bring to a victorious issue only with the assistance of the men. She remains inactive until her own misery—perhaps in consequence of the loss of her supporter—forces her to reflect on the necessity of opening for woman ways upon which she might obtain what she needs, and what no one is likely to give her of his own free will.

There are even cases in which the wife holds

back the husband from entering the movement in favor of women. That is a fatal mistake. In my opinion, there is no nobler and higher calling for woman than to live for her family in the true sense of the word, and no one deserves greater reverence than a mother who is to her children what she should be. But just because of my reverence for the German housewife, as she should be, for the woman who not only educates her daughters, but is also able to guard the interests of her husband and her adult sons, I would protest against the superstition, that the housewife and the scientifically educated woman are incongruities which threaten to rend German life in twain. For the wife who does not understand the great interests of her husband is not able to foster and increase his idealism which disdains material for higher gains, she will, on the contrary, endeavor to drag him down to her low level.

It is said that the best in woman is something quite different from knowledge. That is very true. And if she had not this best and had all the wisdom and intelligence on earth, she would be but like the proverbial "sounding brass and tinkling cymbal." This expression is more applicable to woman than to man. I go still further. There are exceptional cases in whom a sort of intuition seems to compensate for knowledge wanting; who from the depth of their own inner self derive revelations which to others can only come from without. Happy are those who come into contact with such people. Such beings are found among men also; I only need to mention Pestalozzi. But these exceptional cases are much rarer than is commonly taken for granted as regards women, of whom it is customary to say that they hit upon everything with this sort of intuition. For the average woman a thorough education is just as necessary, and exactly as valuable, as for the man, even if we leave out of consideration the pressing need which urges her to obtain it. What it may mean for both, always provided they possess that one *sine qua non* that I believe to have sufficiently emphasized in the foregoing arguments. Those err who think education is able to do everything for the man but nothing for the woman.

The fear of a thorough education of women is in Germany specifically modern; the Middle Ages did not entertain it. Our modern time has created the "blue-stocking" because it refused higher knowledge to women and thus increased the demand for it till it became morbid and led to all kinds of eccentricities. Women, then, who are inclined toward a certain intellectual indolence are apt to cause the opinion in their husbands that women really have no time for any serious study, and that it would scarcely be advisable for them to attempt it. This makes them disinclined to aid in the intellectual liberation of women, being taught to believe that this would estrange them from their true vocation. Since I have seen the much occupied wife of a clergyman (whose house was never without visitors, who had several children of her own and a large number of foster children, and yet contrived to look after their wants) spend an hour every noon in serious scientific study, not in novel reading; since I know that it is possible to the housewife of the present, even under the most difficult circumstances, to foster her intellect, experience has taught me that women who are constantly at work in forming their intellectual world are best adapted to fulfill their duties as housewives and mothers.

Perhaps the circumstances mentioned are the causes of the fact why we Germans have no Henry Sidgwick, no Dr. Anstie, and no Thomas Holloway.

And yet, though we can mention but few men who have actively advocated our cause (one of these few has been President Lette), the number of those who would raise their voice for us, and who have justice enough to acknowledge our claims and the necessity for their final allowance, is increasing steadily. I have the great pleasure of quoting one, in order to show our German women that we need not despair of the assistance of thoroughly educated men. The movement in favor of better professional education of female teachers has shown us that last year.

Clemens Nohl speaks in his "Pedagogy for Higher Schools" of the absolute necessity to grant the female sex a thorough education, and says the mother needs it for the sake of her family, the unmarried woman for her own sake.

"That the maiden is destined to become wife and mother is a proposition that sounds rational and natural, but the world treats it very impolitely and inconsiderately. Of course this destiny is all right if the maiden finds a man who can support her and a family, one who is worthy of her respect and love, as she is of his. Otherwise this destiny is as vague as is the destiny of man to virtue, health, wealth, happiness. . . . But a girl who does not find an honest and well-to-do man will have to become her own supporter, and in that case it can not be doubtful that a good school education will in many cases greatly assist an aspiration that is often dictated by inexorable need. And if the state and city authorities (who understand the requirements of the time) have for many a century established institutions of learning, from the lowest special school up to the university, in which young men can partly or entirely prepare themselves for their future professions, why should not the young women set up the same claim?

"Or shall in Germany, where, in centuries gone by, girls and women were so highly honored, and where even now the educated woman enjoys the undiminished respect belonging to her—I mean, shall it be attended with material and moral dangers in Germany to be born a girl? If educated parents can not bequeath wealth to their children —and that is the rule—shall the girls who have not found husbands (and such cases increase from year to year) eat the bread of charity in the homes of relations? Shall they complain, aloud or secretly, that they can be of no use to mankind because mankind disdains their services, though rendered willingly, and refuses to offer their intellect opportunities for application? Shall they give themselves up to shallow or even immoral novels, or become unamiable gossips, because they have not learned to occupy their minds? Shall they morally go to ruin in the maelstrom of life?

"There are few institutions of learning requiring a certain degree of education in which woman can not accomplish acceptable results; and the privilege which the male sex claimed in most branches, and in part still claims, is, if examined closely, a most unjust one. Among these branches is, first of all, the profession of teaching. Since Pestalozzi discovered in the mother the natural teacher and educator and raised woman to high honor in this important activity the employment of female teachers has become a live question, and will not disappear until the equality of the sexes has become an accomplished fact in the profession. . . . The time is not very remote in which male teachers will be employed in schools for boys, and female teachers almost exclusively in schools for girls.

"A man can not have as clear a comprehension of the nature of girls as a woman, a representative of the same sex, undoubtedly has. He is more apt to make mistakes in treating them. Furthermore, in things essentially feminine in female education, such as fostering the sense of order, punctuality, cleanliness, graceful carriage of the body, propriety, and good manners, he can not nearly so well give advice and exercise supervision as a female teacher, with whom such things are matters of course. Again, the very essential factor of education, personal example, is almost wholly excluded, because woman has to practice, partly, at least, different virtues from those of man, and the same virtues not infrequently appear in different forms in the two sexes. To employ young unmarried male teachers in classes full of budding girls and girls growing into maturity is objectionable from a pedagogical and even a moral point of view, which it is unnecessary to discuss here. Older teachers are often lacking in that vivacity in instruction which girls need often in a greater degree than boys and youths.

"It is true, there are male teachers who, with girls of all ages, succeed admirably and exercise a wholesome influence upon them; and, on the other hand, there are female teachers who accomplish nothing good, and even exercise a baneful influence. But frequently male teachers in girls' schools lacking the qualities mentioned before will secure the respect of their pupils by strict discipline which necessitates frequent punishment (and this sooner makes girls unmanageable than boys), or they are teased and cheated by cunning pupils without being aware of it, while in schools in which chiefly female teachers are employed cases of discipline are rare, provided these teachers are professionally well qualified, and instruction and education proceed with less noise and friction. Very often the intercourse between teachers and pupils in such schools is permeated with the spirit of confidence and love.

"That female teachers are not inferior to men in the faithful discharge of duty, that they are punctual in attendance, thorough in daily preparation of their lessons, and equally conscientious in correcting written work at home, . . . all that is not disputed. . . . Great weight also has the opinion of the Imperial Medical Commission, . . . which publishes the fact that the women are not inferior to men in physical endurance.

"Comparative statistics of absence of male and female teachers from school might give surprising results.

"Now, considering that there are fifty thousand elementary teachers* employed in Prussia, the question will at once arise: Are they really all following a *natural calling?* Are they all called? Or are there not, on the contrary, very many among them who have either no talent or no inclination for their profession, or perhaps lack both? Similar conditions, perhaps, appear among the teaching forces in the secondary institutions, where a large number of the scientific teachers, numbering thousands, are employed, so that here,

---

* Seventy-five thousand in 1886–'87, according to the official report.

too, we might meet many who exercise a weak or even baneful influence in education as well as in instruction. We stand here face to face with facts and institutions which can not be more preposterous. Because male teachers who are fit for the profession can not be had in sufficient number, unfit ones are taken to fill all the vacancies! . . . And yet, women might be had in whom skill and talent for teaching and educating children is inborn—at least as many as are found among men. There are thousands of useful women teachers by whom the vacancies might be filled; but no, they are excluded in favor of useless men, and that, too, from girls' schools.

"This revolting injustice, this coarse and vulgar favoritism shown the stronger sex may have been excusable at a time when the female sex had not yet given tangible proofs of its fitness for the teaching profession, and while great numbers of well-educated and cultured young ladies were not as yet obliged by dire necessity to support themselves in some way; but since their usefulness for many years has been proved incontestably in a number of institutions of learning, and even the most obstinate stupidity begins to acknowledge the necessity of self-support on the part of many women, both, state and communities, must at last consent to measure both sexes by the same standard in the question at issue. . . . In the lower grades of the elementary schools, in which no doubt boys and girls can be taught simultaneously, male and female teachers should both be employed. Not the sex, but the serviceableness should decide here. In the higher grades of elementary schools the sexes should be separated more than is done at present, and the girls be given over to female teachers exclusively. In all the classes of girls' high schools (or girls' academies, or whatever the name of these secondary institutions may be) female teachers are preferable, and the employment of men, even in the highest classes, should not be tolerated. Talented men now teaching there may find employment in boys' schools, where they may take the place of unfit teachers, and the latter make themselves useful in other domains of labor. . . .

"Such an increase in the employment of women would not only give thousands of talented, spirited young ladies who are obliged to support themselves, opportunities to find an occupation suitable for their talents and powers, but it would unquestionably improve the entire system of instruction in lower and higher institutions of learning. . . .

"But there are other occupations in which the female sex is fully equal to the male sex; to these belongs the postal, telegraph, and railroad services. It is asserted, though, that in these occupations women have been tried many times, and that these trials had proved them unfit, and that the chiefs of the different postal, telegraph, and railroad bureaus are not inclined to make the experiment again. Should this be true, the question would naturally arise (and it arises despite the great and well-known merits which these men have earned in their respective departments) whether these experiments were made with all due impartiality and without precipitation, and whether these high officials were not influenced by prejudices in passing judgment on the women. . . . Or are the women in France and Belgium, where they are found in great numbers in the most varied positions of responsibility and trust, cleverer and more trustworthy than with us?

"If in previous pages the assertion has been repeatedly made that certain fields of human activity might gain by the employment of female labor, we now wish to express the conviction that improved education—and through that improved usefulness of the female sex—would enable the latter to participate in the great civilizing activity of our time, to help in liberating mankind, in enlightening it in regard to religion and morality, and even act as propelling forces in social and political life. . . . The serious as well as the minor problems of civilization and culture are becoming more numerous and complicated. Hitherto only half the human race, the male sex, has worked at their solution; hence that solution has been in many cases insufficient and one-sided. The time has come in which the other half, equal in intellectual power and supplementing the former, should assist in solving them." *

Thanks and honor to the man, who possesses ideality enough to deny himself the advantages his sex gives him to do homage to truth!

I have quoted him at length for a purpose. A better statement of the case can not be offered, and it is doubly valuable coming from a man. It has cost me some self-denial not to quote his remarks concerning the last point, the task woman could perform in civilization and culture. But it may suffice to merely call attention to the works of Nohl, which in every part deserve the most careful consideration on account of their clearness and undaunted love of truth, for which their author merits the highest honor. Nohl's writings are most valuable, especially for people who are

---

* Paedagogik fuer hoehere Lehranstalten, Clemens Nohl, I Theil, p. 749.

interested in the present efforts for reform in education.*

Though it can not be denied, leaving some few scattered male advocates of our cause out of consideration, that the men in general are guilty of retarding the woman question in Germany; that they frequently, from prejudice, professional jealousy, or ignorance and indifference, block the ways the women offer to walk, it is, on the other hand, equally true that we women bear a great deal of the guilt ourselves. The sins of omission and commission of many married women have been mentioned. It is reasonable to hope that the near future will witness an improvement in that direction, since the present generation hears the momentous question discussed before marrying, and perhaps learns something of its vital importance from dire experience. As yet it is, in comparison with the population, an insignificant number of German women who can not be turned away from their object in view. Many of those who would like to accomplish something, dislike the necessary means, or feel satisfied at having approached the goal half-

---

* Until recently, three parts of his Paedagogik have appeared: Part I. Institutions of learning. Part II. Methods for the different branches of study. Part III. Training of teachers of science.

way. Some are silent from fear of finding displeasure among the men; but he who dislikes to displease will never effect reforms.

I am among the last who would resent a want of self-confidence and consistency in the oppressed, timid sex.* Man often finds it difficult to think out his thoughts in all their consequences, how much more woman under such circumstances! Time will gradually bring a change, extend the horizon, and strengthen the timid. But when want of self-confidence or short-sightedness assumes the form of a public protest against the training of female teachers, as it did repeatedly during the teachers' congress in Weimar last year, the interest of the cause demands that it be resented. Though many things, such as the application of the Biblical word, "And he shall rule over thee," condemn themselves. This idea has found its proper reply in contributions found in Die Lehrerin (The Female Teacher), edited by Mrs. Loeper-Housselle. And if there are really female teachers who still consider such thorough training as I demand for them in the

---

* It is to be regretted that this timidity goes so far as to prevent an immediate reply to the public disparagement of our sex that took place during the meeting of the congress in Eisenach, Oct. 1–4, 1888, where of all the women present not one arose to protest energetically, though doubtless all felt the affront keenly.

foregoing pages objectionable and unnecessary, they condemn themselves also, despite the applause it has found in educational journals.

Also the protests in the name of womanliness do not disturb my conscience. Womanliness! Beautiful, maltreated word! Oh, how much does it signify — love, confidence, idealism, courage for the greatest sacrifice and greatness of soul! And how is it that these people would define it? As prudishness and affectation!

If women shrink from the unaccustomed problems which our time offers, I shall not blame them for it, but those who are unable to cope with them should write, if write they must, only in the name of their own incapacity, and not make remarks which can only have reference to the education of the present generation of women, and hence only fortify the position of man. I am glad to meet them with the courageous word of Helene Adelmann: "I feel that if I were allowed to concentrate my entire energy as a teacher upon one branch I could cope with any man. If there is a woman who does not feel that she can accomplish the highest and best, she should not deny others the strength to do it, provided they remain within the limits of pure womanliness." Here we applaud.

But I have to reply to another accusation, one

which was raised against me publicly. I have been accused of want of gratitude.

Gratitude! Oh, I like to be grateful; but I do not quite comprehend for what. We owe everything to man, I am told. If we were to count up, many items might be placed on our credit page. A woman's care and unfathomable love surround man from the cradle to his grave; she provides his comforts and the leisure he needs for his undisturbed intellectual work. From the beginning of the world the women have attended to the wants of men, have freed them from annoying material cares, have done the hardest slave's service for them in ancient times, and gone through the life of martyrs without murmuring. This being so, we are obliged to view woman's condition historically. How did that condition arise? Natural inclination does not suffice to explain it. Ancient history reveals such a frightful degree of barbarism that not the least doubt can be entertained of the truth of the statement that the right of the stronger decided the position of women. With the right of physical strength man forced woman to render services as he pleased. But he gave her an equivalent in form of support as father, husband, brother, or guardian. The times were so barbaric and manners so brutal that we can not imagine the position of woman in those ages without a personal protector and supporter. That the man should have derived the right of guardianship from his duty of protection and support was quite natural. Unknown were reasons of a higher kind which might have hindered him from exercising this right of guardianship which in its origin was nothing but the right of the stronger. Yet it is plain, and quite consistent with the development of the cause, that the guardianship should cease with the disappearance or discontinuance of the support. Now if at present a great number of German women are obliged to depend upon themselves for their own support, it seems quite unfair that man, who has ceased to be their support and who is not their protector, should still exercise guardianship over them in regard to their education and professional activity. This "historical guardianship" has resulted in hindering the women who are not supported and protected by man from supporting themselves in a way corresponding to their desires and capacities. He prescribes for them an education as he sees fit, an education which is entirely incongruous with their own claims and needs. I can not possibly find in that a cause for gratitude.

But willingly, and with all my heart, will I be grateful to those men who help the women gain the liberty of that education which legal and ideal considerations would suggest. The starting point of woman's present position was, as stated before, man's physical strength. Now, in the same proportion in which the respect for physical superiority recedes and respect for moral qualities increases, in exactly the same proportion will man everywhere voluntarily renounce the guardianship so intimately connected with physical superiority, for nothing except this respect can induce him to do so. And I confidently believe that the German women deserve it as well as the women of other nations. No one is more zealous in praising the women than the Germans, from Walter von der Vogelweide up to the present day. But I believe the time has come to prove this respect by deeds. The boy, when grown to manhood, should recollect the infinite love and care which his mother bestowed upon him; he should prove his gratitude by assisting her sex to obtain that position to which it has an inborn right. Woman, I should think, might be credited now with that degree of intellectual maturity which enables her to decide what is good for herself. And if she desires more intellectual food, more efficacious labor than hitherto, man should not obstinately refuse it. If a tribe of savages showed the degree of intelligence now manifested by the German women, would

LUKEWARM AND HALF-HEARTED WOMEN.

not the men with great willingness open their universities for them? Would not every German professor contribute his share to induce the "cultivable tribe" (*bildungsfähigen Stamm*) to acquire the highest intellectual culture for which it is aspiring? Does any one think the case possible that this tribe should again and again vainly petition for admission to European culture and be repulsed with derision and disgrace? Every educated man would declare it despicable narrow-mindedness, and consider it a burning shame.

Yet exactly the same thing is done with the German women, because they *are* women; for no other reason. Why, then, should we feel such deep gratitude toward the German men, and not venture to criticise the institutions made by them?

But let us return to the women.

Though during the public discussion of the woman question, which grows more and more urgent, it is found that there are some women in Germany who belong to the lukewarm and half-hearted, to the short-sighted and timid, and that the co-operation is wanting which has led to excellent results in other countries, still it would be unjust not to recognize gladly that on the other hand the number of women is steadily increasing who are independent yet womanly in the true sense of the word, and who are consistent in thought and action. And there is no doubt that these women will in the course of time find the proper appreciation among the doubting and timid of their sex, who are not as yet aware of their own strength. In that the pioneers must find comfort. How willingly, how gladly one is a pioneer for a great and pure cause like the intellectual elevation and liberation of a whole sex. This joyful prospect will take the sting out of the depressing consciousness that this pioneer work has been performed here by courageous women for twenty-five years without the great results achieved in other countries. It helps one forget a little, too, that one is personally misjudged.

But it has been thought necessary to warn the German nation to beware of these pioneers. "These women," it is said, "aim at a total revolution of the social position of the educated woman."

What does this really mean? Are we by the term social position to understand the position of woman in human society and professional life in general? Then it is perfectly correct. We are trying with the aid of thorough-bred gentlemen to cause a change in the social position of woman. We wish to secure to woman the same liberty for her intellectual education that man has, and that will necessitate a dislocation and readjustment in professional life by replacing some incapable men by capable women; for the question of capability has always been placed in the foreground by us, since it alone can decide the contest. Hence capable men need not fear anything. A warning, such as that alluded to, would only be a consequence of premises easily guessed. But if by the term social position the position of woman in relation to man, that is, to her husband, is understood, nothing need be feared from a higher education and an elevation of her position as wife resulting therefrom; for the position of the wife in regard to her husband is not at all dependent upon his superiority. The inner superiority is not by any means always on the side of the husband either; in the lower strata of society, where the degree of school education is equal, it is not even found in education. If, nevertheless, woman serves man in innumerable ways, makes his life pleasant and comfortable, and if her life is an "eternal coming and going, a lifting and bearing, a working and caring for others," it is because love and the exigences of her nature impel her to it; and that will always be so whether she reads Marlitt or Sophocles in her leisure hours, else I but poorly understand woman's nature. But where remnants of that ancient oppression are still practiced, where to woman are offered, with legal sanction, all kinds of ignominies, she is quite right to attempt to find redress. It is to be hoped that she will find the assistance of noble-spirited men who will secure to her the legal protection needed against her husband's abuse of power. The better part of married life, as it is slowly assuming form in all civilized countries, is based upon affection, hence is safe from all attempts at emancipation. The attempts we are making are invariably directed toward breaking unjust barriers which are set up to prevent woman from obtaining intellectual culture and increasing her professional capacity; they are not aimed at a change of her position in married life. Only coarse people will try to escape from duties, the fulfillment of which the woman's position necessitates, and in that they will never find support among true women. These will never think of denying their husbands with what love has provided him from time immemorial. Only the men must not believe they can demand as a tribute due their alleged superiority what love alone can give and will give willingly, plentifully, and forevermore.

And where is the movement to end? Exactly where the nature of the case and the nature of woman will demand that it should end. No one should think of being able to arrest it, nor need any one apprehend dangers where Nature is simply allowed to speak; she will erect barriers sufficiently high to check anything she can not sanction. After woman has been "declared of age" the future will in all probability take this form: As in the past, the majority of women will live for their families and endeavor to make home happy and comfortable; Nature guarantees that. Later on, a number of married women whose inclination and circumstances induced them in youth to pursue more serious studies than is now the custom—perhaps with the view of an eventual professional application—will (even if this necessity does not arise) have reason to be well satisfied with the interest their intellectual labor will yield them. Their deeper comprehension of interests for which they formerly had only sympathies because people whom they loved pursued them, their more extended horizon, and their deeper insight into the aims and aspirations of husband and sons—all that can only benefit the home life. Unmarried women will select the same professional occupations they now select; but a few more will be added to the number of eligible occupations to which those women will aspire who are capable enough to enter into competition with men, and, of course, they will reach the same satisfactory, distinguished, and lucrative position that the men occupy at present. Among the learned professions the medical and teacher's profession will be chosen by women. The possibility of obtaining a secure and lucrative position by one's own strength will undoubtedly prevent many marriages which nowadays are entered into from fear of privation, or because not to be married is considered a disgrace—in other words, marriages will be prevented which are based on immoral foundations. Hence, looked at from this side, married life and family life can only gain. The fact also that the daughters of the house would in school be under the guidance and influence of women exclusively would indirectly aid family life.

Thus, to an unprejudiced eye, the future appears not as the caricature of a world, in which cigarettes and torn clothes are considered attributes of woman. A part of this caricature might, however, become reality if opposition to the development that has become necessary is continued much longer. For the longer and the more violently anything is opposed that Nature dictates, the more objectionable and hazardous become the hybrid forms which the misapplied strength causes in all directions. The female life in Germany is a healthy one throughout; if, however, the liberty of development that has become so necessary is denied it, the consequences will not be wanting. They will be much more dangerous than the consequences of "emancipation," a word that has become a veritable apparition. Like all ghosts, this too will prove a mere phantom. The events in other countries have proved this clearly. In most of them liberty of development has been granted woman after some contention, but as soon as the fight ended the unpleasant features of emancipation, being only sequences of unjustified opposition, disappeared. A fact which is very striking in England is that the women who stand in the midst of the movement and practice so-called male professions are thoroughly womanly women. No doubt in Germany the strong opposition will cause occasional unpleasant results. Up to date but few German women have acquired a higher education in foreign countries. If they intend to acquire it in Germany they meet with the greatest obstacles; they have to go through an almost exhausting fight with ill-will and prejudices, and though this does not always injure their womanly qualities, in some of them is noticeable an indefinable something which savors of a consciousness of their exceptional position. It is true that position was gained by summoning all available energy and by removing many obstacles. (We have every reason to be proud of the representatives of our sex who in Berlin practice so-called male professions.) They are phenomena and feel it. The battles through which they passed have left an impression on their characters, and their conduct shows it. Naturally, this being something that comes to the surface, it is noticed, and the opponents of the woman's movement make good use of the fact. That is, however, unavoidable in the infancy of a cause. The Germans, for instance, are at present conscious of being a nation, a distinction for which they bitterly fought, and hence are tempted to some exaggerations; likewise, the women who had to go through, and victoriously passed, examinations that raised them to the lofty height of the upper ten thousand in spirit, are apt to show it a little in their conduct. But such emotions will soon disappear when to have a university education ceases to be an exception. If we would avoid the small-pox we must not shrink from the trifling vaccination fever. If we want to prevent serious social injuries, if we intend to leave unfilled the intellectual chasm that now separates the world of man from the world of woman in Germany and makes an agreement so difficult, occasional childish conduct, attributable to the state of tutelage in which woman had been left, must be taken into the bargain. But those who speak of serious dangers for the German family that are alleged to arise from a change of the social position

of woman do not know woman at all, or if they do
they use such arguments as a cloak for other and
meaner motives.

The same holds true with those who point
toward serious dangers to the bodily health of woman arising from an extension of her sphere of
activity. The Cologne Gazette (October 11, 1888)
contains this passage: "In Berlin a great number of
weary, gray, old women of scarcely thirty years
creep about in the attempt at acquiring a man's
education; all vivacity of feeling, all womanly emotions, and physical health besides has left them.
Truly educated and cultured men avoid them, uneducated ones flee them [If that is to be a weighty
argument it is of very light weight], and the healthy
natural women shun their society. Thus these girls
stand like hermaphrodites between the two sexes."

At first reading, one is inclined to laugh over
this unmitigated nonsense, especially when one
lives in Berlin and looks in vain for "creeping,
weary, old women of scarcely thirty." But no, not
quite in vain. We see such old women; pale, hollow-chested sewing girls and factory hands, poor
working women leading emaciated children by the
hand, and by them we are reminded at every step
of an unpaid debt of society. We also see rich
women who while away their days in fancy pleas-

ures, women whose heads are empty and whose hearts are dead. But among the intellectually hard-working women I personally know not a single one who could be classed among the decrepit old women. It is possible that there are a few, and it would be astonishing if there were none under the *present* circumstances. And then the reply would suggest itself, why should not a woman have the right to ruin her health in pursuing intellectual studies or devoting herself to a satisfying and remunerative profession, as well as a sewing girl or a factory hand, or a woman in the whirl of society? But there is still another reply: *If* she is ruining her health, what else is the cause but the fact, that she is obliged to work ten times harder than might be necessary because the assistance offered to men is denied her?

If, as the author of that article in the Cologne Gazette says, she fills her head with facts from all branches of science without ever finding the connecting link in any one science, what else is the cause but that she is denied assistance and limited by uncertain means? How difficult it is to find the connecting link, even when such assistance is given, is shown in the article mentioned above, the author of which is incapable of analyzing primary and secondary causes. If the "imbittered woman," upon whom the author looks down with the feeling of the proverbial Pharisee, becomes deeply unhappy, it is not owing to her intellectual aspirations, for her aspiration is as high and as pure as —say, as that of man; but it is owing to the fact that she is everywhere rejected with her claim upon work, useful work; not even for the education and instruction of her own sex is she taken into consideration in earnest. No wonder if she becomes imbittered. There is but one thing which does imbitter—vain aspiration for work and usefulness.

All of us whom kind, motherly Nature has equipped with tenacity to hold our ground in battling with adverse circumstances, who stand in the midst of a professional life that fills our heart, let us never cease fighting for our imbittered sisters, upon whom only men without education, hence without culture, can look down with derision. She who wants nothing for herself may demand everything for others.

For the present I am done with what I had to say. I have said it in my simple way, without much circumlocution, since I am wanting in the power of framing my thoughts in rhetorical figures. I have only this desire—that my words be accepted as sincere and honest; they certainly are meant to be so. And, above all, I should like to have them examined without prejudice. I know well enough that those who have cause to fear a change, not feeling themselves able to cope with it, will protest with all their weight in the name of the "good olden times," in the name of the family, or, perchance, in the name of German science; but I appeal to the sense of justice and sound judgment of all independently thinking German men. For their benefit, I repeat Ludwig Schwerin's words: "The narrow limit within which the so-called weaker sex is kept is the result of prejudice inherited from our forefathers; it is human ordinance, physiologically and psychologically unfounded, a mixture of heathenish-antique and Christian-scholastic views of the world. Generation after generation passes by careless and indifferent to the wrong done to woman. That which in woman is noble and tender can never be injured by genuine, true education and its resultant, the highest culture known."

THE END.

www.ingramcontent.com/pod-product-compliance
Lightning Source LLC
Chambersburg PA
CBHW021013240426
43669CB00037B/1050